Prefab Houses DesignSource

Marta Serrats

HARPER
DESIGN
An Imprint of HarperCollins Publishers

HarperCollins books may be purchased for educational, business, or sales promotional use.
For information, please write: Special Markets Department, HarperCollins*Publishers*,
195 Broadway, New York, NY 10007.

First Edition published in 2012 by
Harper Design
An Imprint of HarperCollins*Publishers*
195 Broadway,
New York, NY 10007
Tel.: (212) 207-7000
Fax: (212) 207-7654
harperdesign@harpercollins.com
www.harpercollins.com

Distributed throughout the world by
HarperCollins*Publishers*
195 Broadway,
New York, NY 10007
Fax: (212) 207-7654

Packaged by
LOFT Publications
Via Laietana 32, 4.º, of. 92
08003 Barcelona, Spain
Tel.: +34 932 688 088
Fax: +34 932 687 073
loft@loftpublications.com
www.loftpublications.com

Editorial coordination: Aitana Lleonart Triquell
Editor: Marta Serrats
Art director: Mireia Casanovas Soley
Design and layout coordination: Claudia Martínez Alonso
Cover layout: María Eugenia Castell Carballo
Layout: Anabel N. Quintana

Translation: Cillero & de Motta

ISBN 978-0-06-211354-2

14 15 16 SCP 10 9 8 7 6 5 4 3 2

Library of Congress Control Number: 2011943950

Manufactured in China

INDEX

INTRODUCTION

Assembly, instead of construction, is an alternative method of house building that is attracting more and more followers, especially in Nordic countries and the United States, where prefabricated modules and *McMansions* are gaining popularity in zones with high seismic risk. The use of factory-produced, prefabricated components that are later assembled on-site is becoming more common. This type of home is defended by many as a solution that speeds up the construction process, and reduces costs and environmental impact.

The concept of the prefabricated home is in line with modular home proposals, whose components have been manufactured in a factory miles away from the final location. The pieces are sold and purchased as a kit, and the end result is usually a one-story, detached, eco-efficient house, built according to sustainable construction criteria. There are also multi-family constructions—housing that uses prefabricated elements such as columns, floors, and roofs, ensuring that the building is constructed in less time. A prefabricated house can be assembled and occupied in a matter of days. This is one of the key arguments in favor of prefabricated architecture: savings in the time needed to build, labor, and materials, resulting in significant economic benefits.

From an environmental point of view, it also reduces construction waste because the prefabricated components are manufactured off-site and consequently generate less waste in the area where the house will be built. Moreover, the fact that the panels can be built earlier allows for the use of energy-efficient products, which provide greater insulation from the interior and a higher quality, without them being exposed to inclement weather during construction.

A new path is opening up in the world of building at a time when the construction industry cannot seem to find a way out of the recent economic crisis. Prefabricated houses make housing more accessible for many people whose main concern is a lower final price. This is a new, environmentally viable, alternative that avoids intensive labor, exorbitant costs, and the use of materials and processes that do damage to the very neighborhoods we're building in.

Prefab Houses DesignSource offers readers the opportunity to view a selection of current prefabricated homes that show the possibility of a new way. If the consumer opts for a prefabricated home with specific technologies and local, low impact materials, which is built with local labor, it not only reduces the ecological footprint, but will mean they acquire a good home at an affordable price.

Hidden Valley House

Architect:
Marmol Radziner Prefab

Location:
Moab, UT, United States

Photos:
© Joe Fletcher

The interior of the house features eco-efficient appliances, a geothermal ventilation control system, and paints that are low in volatile organic compounds (VOCs).

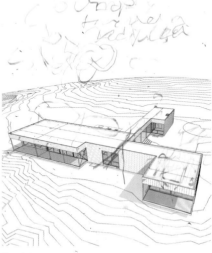

Site plan

13

The main axis of this vacation home runs along a rocky hillside, providing spectacular desert views.

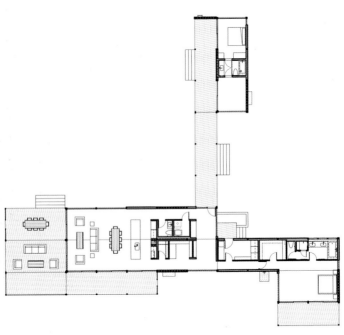

Plan

HUF Fachwerkhaus 2000 ART 9

Architect:
Manfred Adams, Huf Haus

Location:
Hartenfels, Germany

Photos:
© Huf Haus GMBH & Co. KG

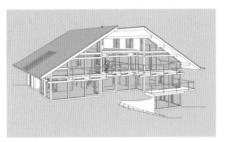

Front view

Rear view

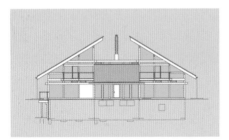

North elevation

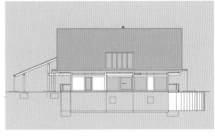

East elevation

The Huf Haus Company sells homes from a catalog. All of their constructions feature bioclimatic designs, environmental technology, and modern lines that blend with their surroundings.

The interiors feature clean surfaces, versatile
spaces, and a feeling of space.

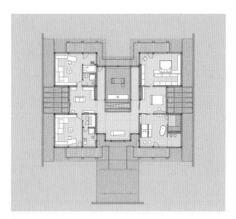

First floor

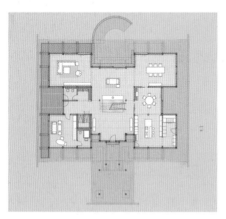

Ground floor

Basement

Farley Studio

Architect:
M. J. Neal Architects

Location:
Cleburne, TX, United States

Photos:
© Viviana Vives, M. J. Neal

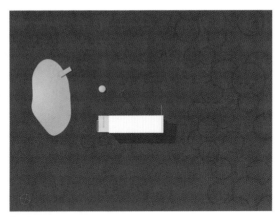

Site plan

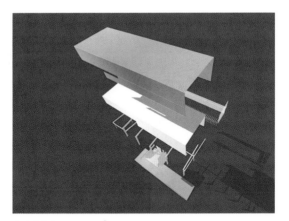

Exploded view

The west wing is clad in a blue glass façade.
The same material was used on the south façade
together with a metal panel that acts as a
protective screeen.

29

By day, the building resembles a simple metal and glass box. By night, the interior appears to levitate behind the polycarbonate panels.

West elevation

North elevation

East elevation

South elevation

The design is bioclimatic: the metal box acts as thermal protection, while the central structure allows cross ventilation.

House S

Architect:
Korteknie Stuhlmacher Architecten

Location:
Charbonnières-les-Bains, France

Photos:
**© Moritz Bernoully, Olivier Nord,
Korteknie Stuhlmacher Architecten**

The outer wall and the roof of the house are made from laminated panels measuring between 3.34 and 11.4 inches in thickness.

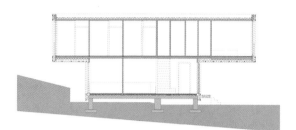

Cross section 1

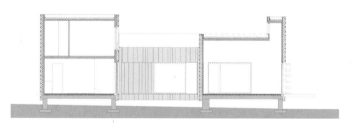

Longitudinal section 1

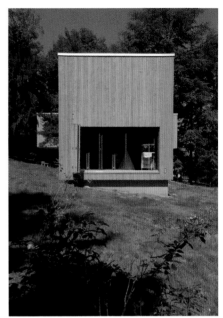

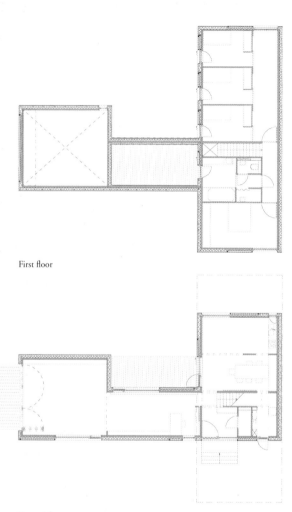

First floor

Ground floor

The architects chose to use natural materials. The
structural frame of the building is made from
prefabricated wood panels.

Glidehouse

Architect:
MKD-Michelle Kaufmann Designs

Location:
Novato, CA, United States

Photos:
© John Swain

Each Glidehouse is prefabricated in a controlled environment and subsequently, transported to the site for assembly. This system reduced building time.

Site plan

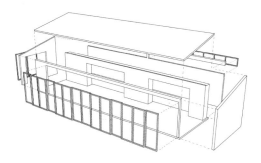

Factory production

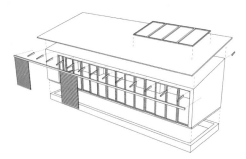

On site button up

Completed glidehouse

The object is to design and build bioclimatic homes using eco-friendly materials and advanced assembly techniques that simplify the building process.

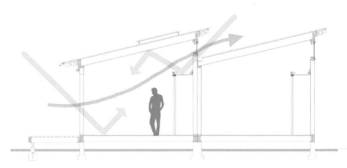

Bioclimatic section

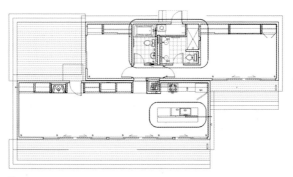

Plan

House Braun-Dubuis

Architect:
Atelier Werner Schmidt

Location:
Disentis, Switzerland

Photos:
© Atelier Werner Schmidt

The second level floor is made of bales of straw, a 4-inch thick layer of concrete, and a covering of stone tiles.

Sketch

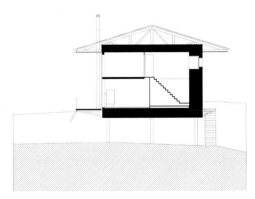

Section A-A

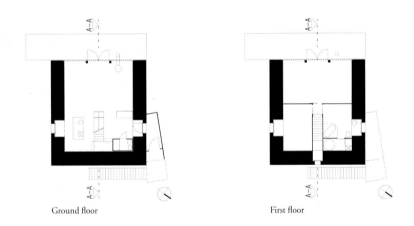

Ground floor

First floor

The main components of the home are concrete and bales of straw, which also act as natural insulation.

Next House Collection Théa

Architect:
Magnus Ståhl

Location:
Stockholm, Sweden

Photos:
© **Christian Saltas**

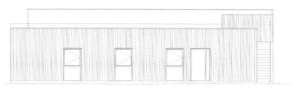

Northeast elevation

Northwest elevation

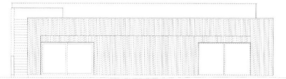

Southwest elevation

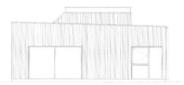

Southeast elevation

Next House has a catalog of prefabricated homes designed by a number of Swedish architects. These come in different shapes and sizes: XXS, S, M, and L.

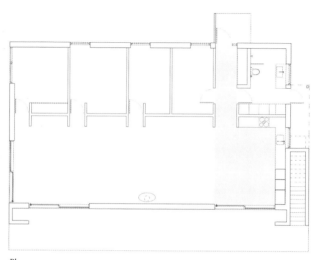

Plan

This 4-bedroom L-category home was designed
for a couple with children.

X House

Architect:
Arquitectura X

Location:
Quito, Ecuador

Photos:
© Sebastián Crespo

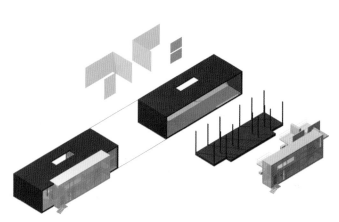

Deconstructed axonometric view

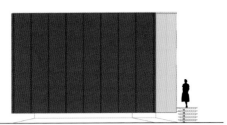

North elevation

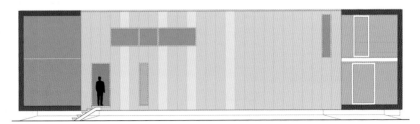

West elevation

The glass volume projects the interior of X House out to the exterior, while the polycarbonate-walled courtyard divides the internal spaces.

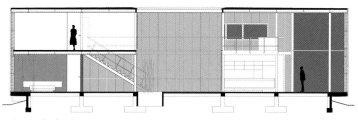

Longitudinal section

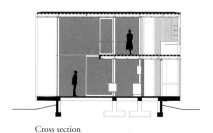

Cross section

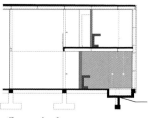

Cross section 2

This house was built using industrial materials including steel, plywood, and polycarbonate. The steel frame is made from prefabricated rectangular sections measuring 20 feet in length.

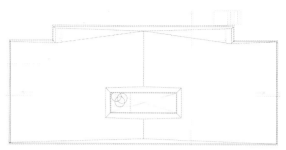

Roof plan

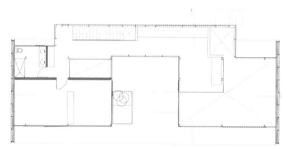

First floor

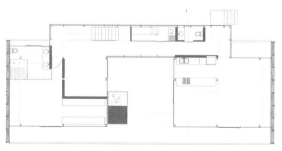

Ground floor

The partition walls are made from sandblasted polycarbonate and glass. The floor of the box is plywood and the prefabricated courtyard has a polished white cement floor.

Modular 4

Architect:
Studio 804

Location:
Kansas City, KS, United States

Photos:
© **Studio 804**

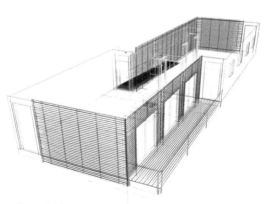

Perspective diagram

The wall and roof insulation of Modular 4 is made out of cellulose fiber from recycled newspapers.

The layout of the openings enhances cross ventilation. The south-facing glass, comprising three sliding doors, optimizes passive solar gain in winter.

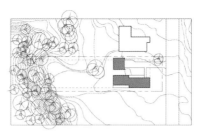

Site plan

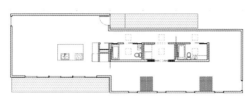

A-Plan

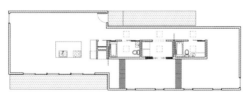

B-Plan

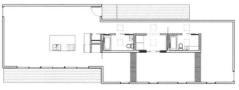

C-Plan

Black Box

Architect:
Matthias R. Schmalohr

Location:
Krainhagen, Germany

Photos:
© **Klaus Dieter Weiss**

The prefabricated parts of this house are the external wood structure and the waterproof plywood, with internal insulation made from cellulose.

Site plan

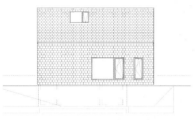

Southeast elevation

Northeast elevation

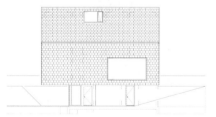

Northwest elevation

Southwest elevation

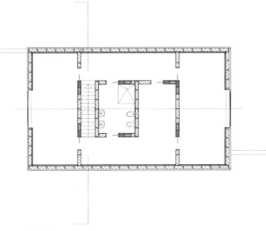

First floor

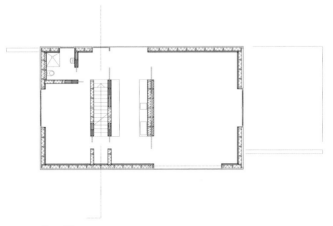

Ground floor

The spaces were designed on three levels: the entrance and cellar in the basement; the living area, study, service areas, and multi-purpose room on the first level; and two bedrooms and a bathroom on the second level.

R.R. House

Architect:
Andrade Morettin Associated Architects

Location:
Itamambuca, São Paulo, Brasil

Photos:
© Nelson Kon

Site plan

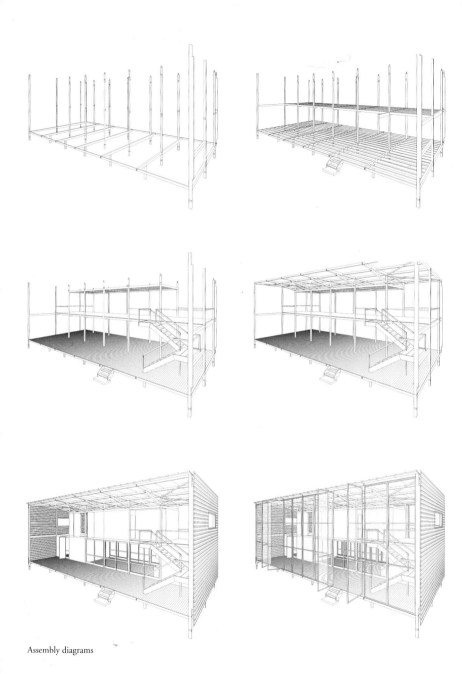

Assembly diagrams

The building's bioclimatic system uses passive energy systems that will reduce its CO_2 emissions during its lifetime.

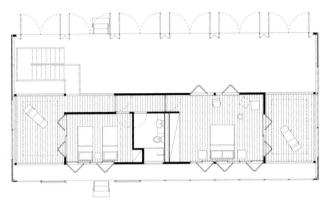

First floor

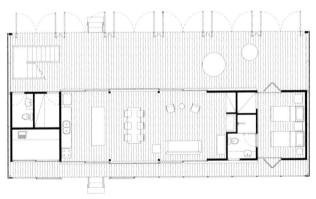

Ground floor

House of Huts

Architect:
Studio NL-D

Location:
Breda, The Netherlands

Photos:
© Hans Werlemann/Hectic Pictures

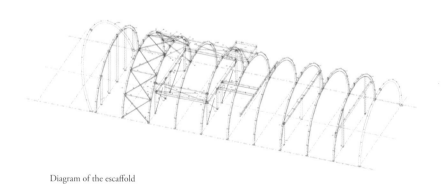

Diagram of the escaffold

The architects of this house decided on a prefabricated solution as a way of cutting costs and shortening construction time. In this case, it only took three months to build.

Section

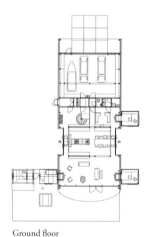

Ground floor

First floor

A climate control system guarantees the perfect inside temperature by means of radiant floors and wall heating.

The Floating House

Architect:
Ronan & Erwan Bouroullec

Location:
Chatou, France

Photos:
© Paul Tahon, Ronan & Erwan Bouroullec

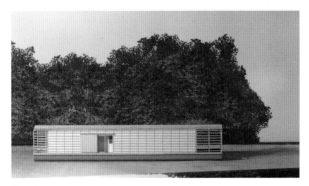

Front view

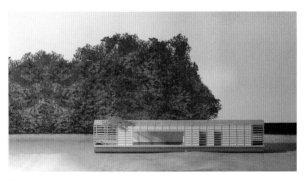

Rear view

Vines were planted,which grew to cover the walls and roof. As a result, the structure blends seamlessly with the landscape while protecting the privacy of its occupants.

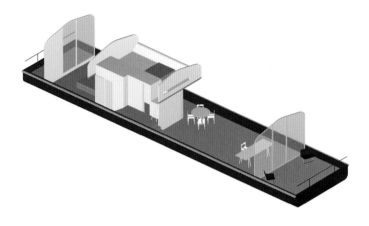

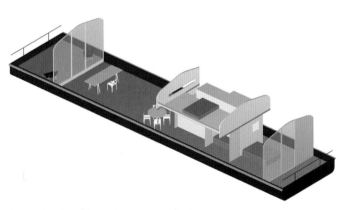

Axonometric view of the interior conpartmentalization

Cape House

Architect:
Resolution: 4 Architecture

Location:
Cape Cod, MA, United States

Photos:
© Joshua McHugh, Resolution: 4 Architecture

Northwest perspective view

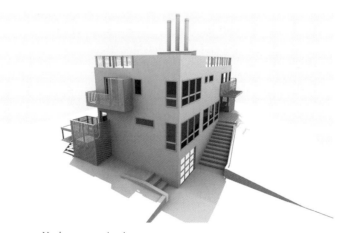

Northeast perspective view

The prefabricated parts of Cape House were transported by truck, as is the case with most prefabricated buildings.

East elevation

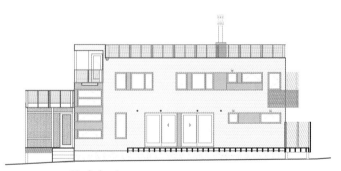

North elevation

The home has a rectangular plan over two levels.
All the rooms have openings to the outside.

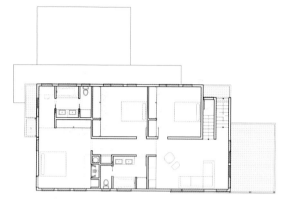

First floor

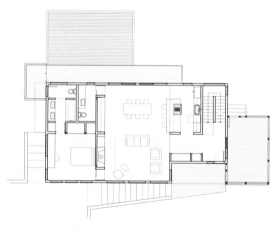

Ground floor

Loblolly House

Architect:
KieranTimberlake Associates

Location:
Taylors Island, MD, United States

Photos:
© Barry Hlakin

Environmental impact was reduced by raising
the building over timber pilings. The outer walls
feature an insulation system that enhances the
thermal efficiency of the interior.

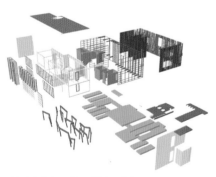

Exploded view wih prefabricated elements

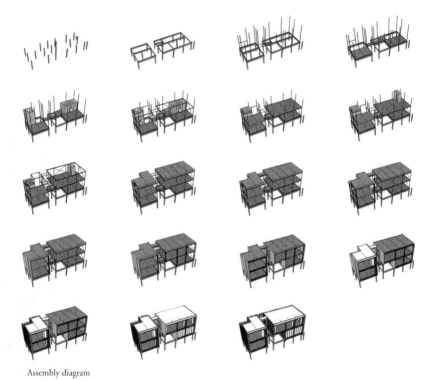

Assembly diagram

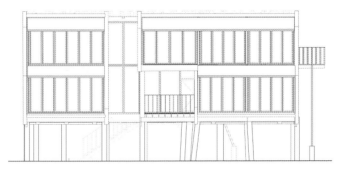

West elevation

South elevation

The basic components of the home are its aluminum frame, fiber cement panels, wood siding, aluminum joinery, and interior finishes made from birch veneer plywood.

Wall House

Architect:
FAR frohn&rojas

Location:
Santiago, Chile

Photos:
© **Cristobal Palma**

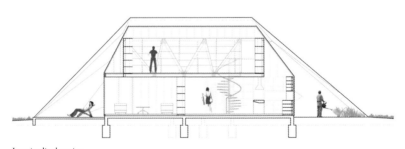

Longitudinal section

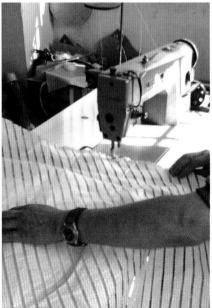

Approximately 70 % of the dwelling is prefabricated, mainly the stacked shelving and the exterior factory-sewn soft skin. It took four days to assemble both elements.

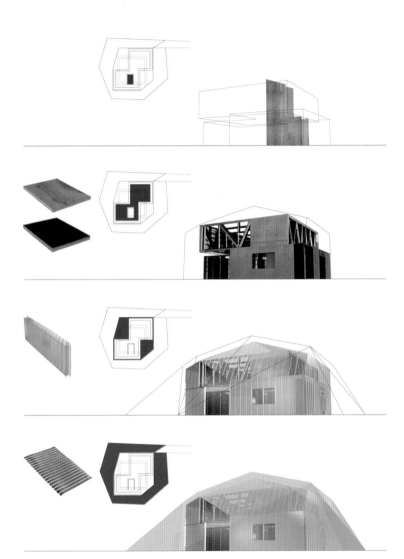

Sketch of construction by layers and materials

The layer formed by the milky shell and double glass, with sliding doors and pivoting glass panels, creates a translucent enveloping layer through which light passes to illuminate the interior spaces.

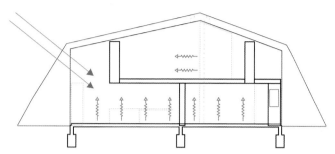

Bioclimatic sketch (winter)

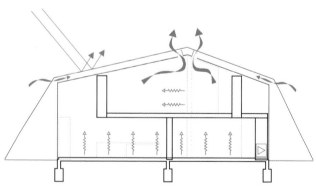

Bioclimatic sketch (summer)

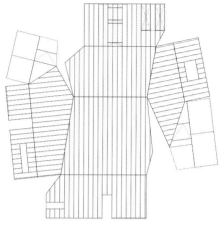

Layer milky shell

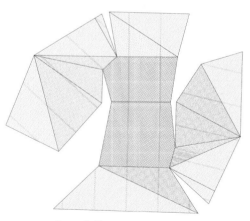

Layer soft skin

M2 Kip House

Architect:
Kim Herforth Nielsen/3XN

Location:
Vindeby, Denmark

Photos:
© Adam Mørk, Kaj Lergaard

Renderings

Black is the central feature of this design: the
wood siding has a black finish and asphalt
membrane was used to waterproof the roof.

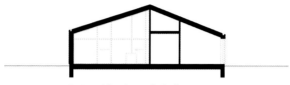

Section of the 1658 sq. ft. dwelling

Section of the 1755 sq. ft. dwelling

Section of the 1938 sq. ft. dwelling

143

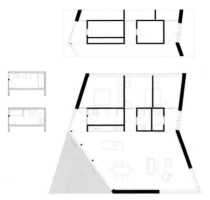

Floor plan of the 1626 sq. ft. dwelling

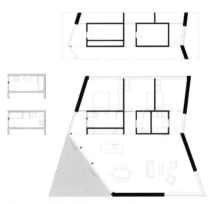

Floor plan of the 1938 sq. ft. dwelling

House M

Architect:
Caramel Architekten

Location:
Linz, Austria

Photos:
© Otto Hainzl/Augment

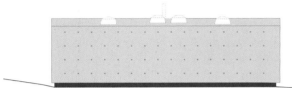

North elevation

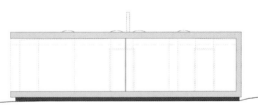

South elevation

The north and west façades are completely
exposed to the exterior through large glazed
expanses, affording the inhabitants views over
the Danube Valley to the west.

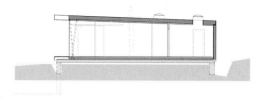

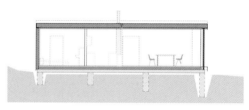

Sections

Plan

Streckhof Reloaded

Architect:
Franz Architekten

Location:
Zellerndorf, Austria

Photos:
© **Lisa Rastl**

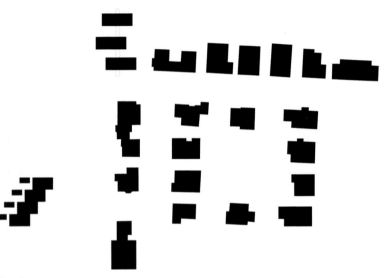

Site plan

This house in Zellerndorf, Austria, consists of three separate units connected by a glass corridor.

Elevation

Longitudinal section

The pool and terrace are among the
volumes furthest from the street and can
be accessed from the kitchen, living room,
corridor, or the parent's bedroom.

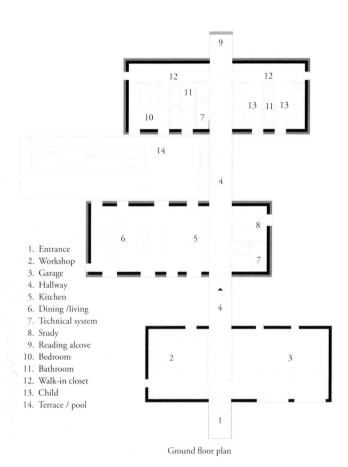

9

12   12

11

13   11   13

10   7

14

4

8

6   5

7

4

2   3

1

1. Entrance
2. Workshop
3. Garage
4. Hallway
5. Kitchen
6. Dining /living
7. Technical system
8. Study
9. Reading alcove
10. Bedroom
11. Bathroom
12. Walk-in closet
13. Child
14. Terrace / pool

Ground floor plan

The three volumes house different
functions, the garage in the area closest to
the street, the living areas in the center,
and the bedrooms in the private unit.

The Number House

Architect:
**Mitsutomo Matsunami Architect
& Associates**

Location:
Ibaraki, Japan

Photos:
**© Mitsutomo Matsunami Architect
& Associates**

Elevation

Floor plans

This row of prefabricated houses is characterized by a façade that looks like a sequence of numbers. The four façades appear as if they were one.

Kyoto House

Architect:
Pich-Aguilera

Location:
Torre Serona, Spain

Photos:
© Jordi V. Pou

This project was built out of concrete in order to benefit from the structure's thermal mass. Low impact insulating materials, such as glass and wool, were also used.

First floor

Roof plan

Ground floor

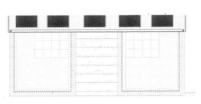

Basement

Residence for a Sculptor

Architect:
Sander Architects

Location:
Santa Rosa, CA, United States

Photos:
© Sharon Risedorph Photography

Sketches

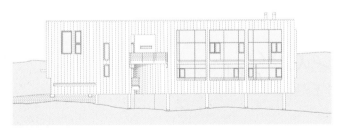

South elevation

Once the useful life of the home comes to an end, its structure can be taken apart and recycled, or reused for another project. The garden contains drought-resistant plant varieties.

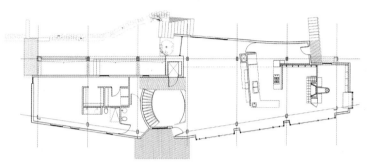

First floor

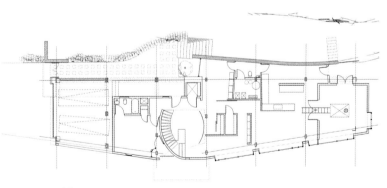

Ground floor

System 3

Architect:
Oskar Leo Kaufmann, Albert Rüf

Location:
**Museum of Modern Art, New York, NY,
United States**

Photos:
© Adolf Bereuter

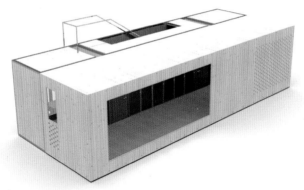

Axonometric view

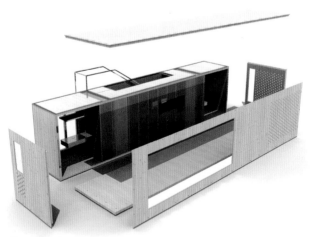

Deconstructed axonometric view

The parts of modular homes fit perfectly inside a shipping container; this means they can be transported by sea or land and assembled at the final location.

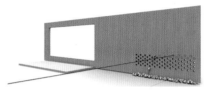

CNC technology-process

CNC technology-finished

Coating

Window

Model 2008
570 sq. ft.
Living area, bedroom, kitchen, bath and roof deck

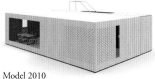

Model 2010
926 sq. ft.
Expanded living area, bedroom, kitchen, bath and roof deck

Model 2016
1496 sq. ft.
Expanded living area, kitchen, bath for guests, master bedroom with bath, bedroom with bath, roofed frontyard/carpot and two roof decks

Model 2028
1711 sq. ft.
Living area, kitchen, bath for guests, master bedroom with bath, bedroom with bath, studio with bath and kitchen on third floor, roofed frontyard/carpot and three roof decks

The structure chosen for MoMA has a smaller layout. There are larger versions with 30 modules that can cover an area of 10,764 sq.ft. and stand 10 stories tall.

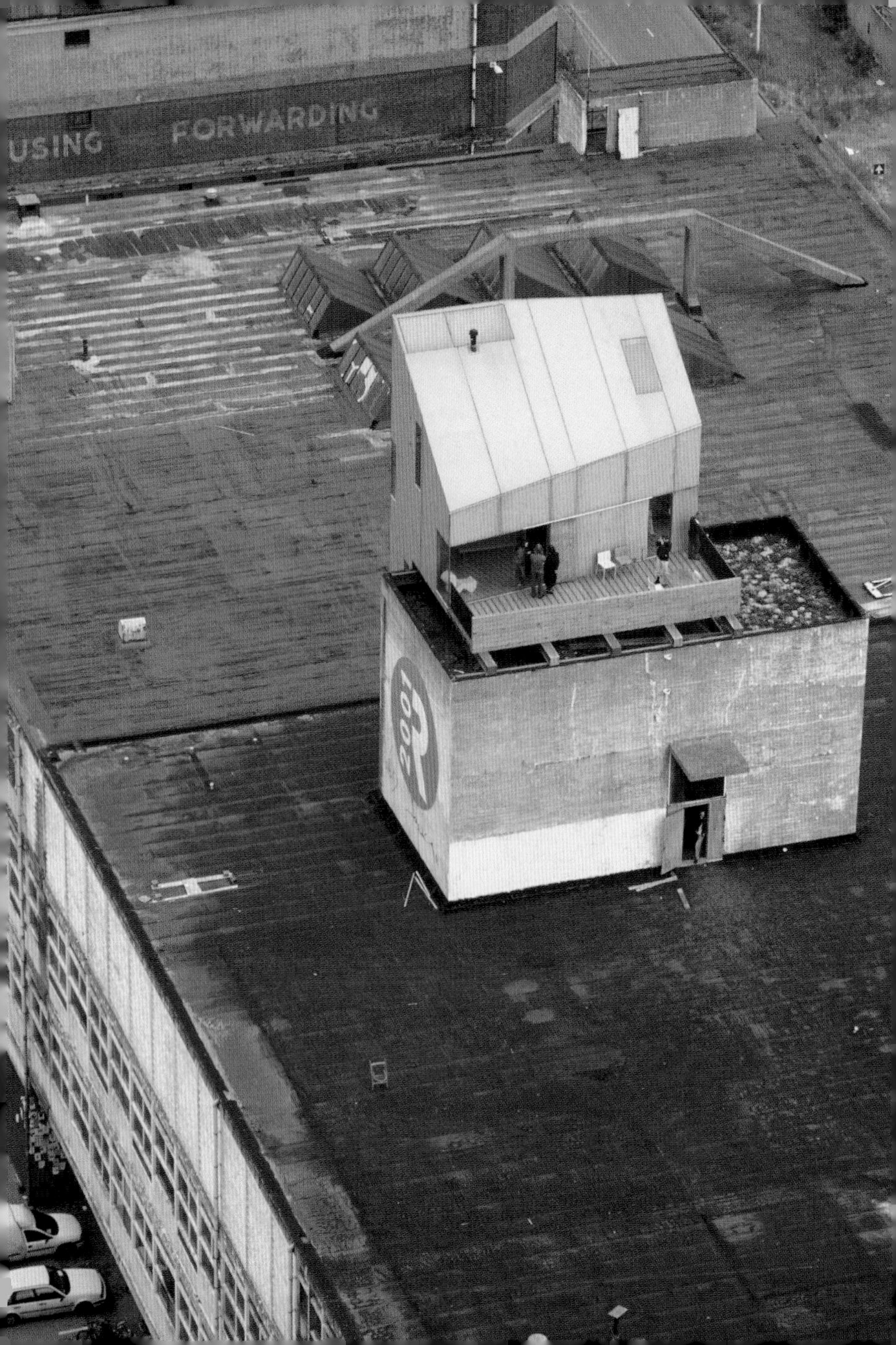
USING
FORWARDING

Parasite Las Palmas

Architect:
Korteknie Stuhlmacher Architekten

Location:
Rotterdam, The Netherlands

Photos:
© **Anne Bousema**

The building emerges like a parasite that is taking over the roof. The prefabricated structure takes advantage of the water and power supplied to the existing building.

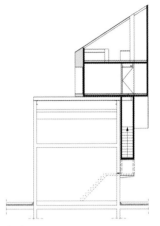

Section

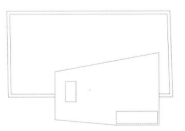

Roof plan

Part of the structural frame is provided by the existing building. The rest was shipped and raised to the roof by crane.

One+

Architect:
Lars Frank Nielsen/ONE N, Add a Room

Location:
Stockholm, Sweden

Photos:
© Matti Marttinen L

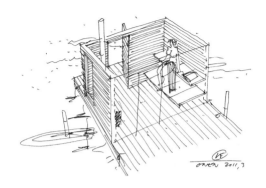

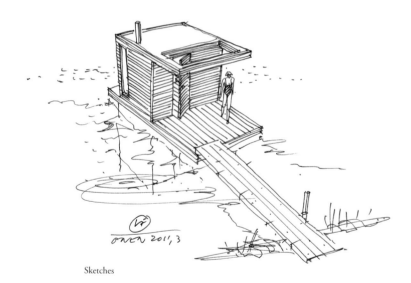

Sketches

This prefabricated home is constructed from 15*m (161ft2) modules that are delivered by truck, completely finished.

The construction is made of highly insulated wooden modules that enable the bathroom, kitchen, and bedrooms to be fitted with beds and closets.

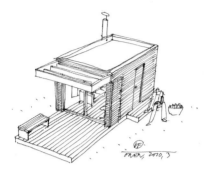

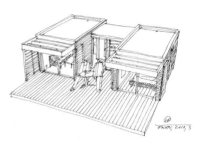

Sketches

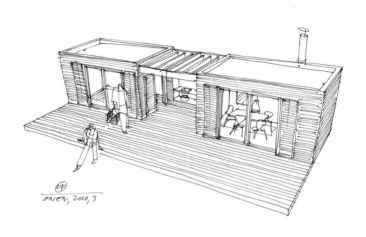

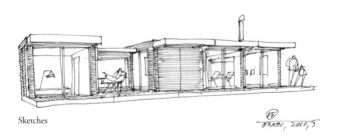

Sketches

Designed as a summer house, the modules allow you to create different compositions that adapt to the user's needs.

The Passive House in Bessancourt

Architect:
Karawitz Architecture

Location:
Bessancourt, France

Photos:
© **Hervé Abbadie**

Elevations

Its structure consists of solid wood panels and is covered with a second skin of untreated bamboo.

Site plan

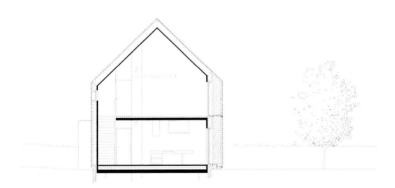

Transversal section

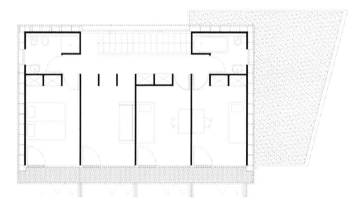

First floor plan

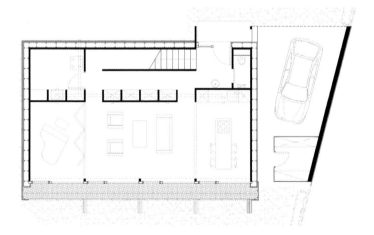

Ground floor plan

The recessed shutters on the south facing windows provide shade or light as required. It has photovoltaic panels that produce 2,695 kWh per year.

Laidley Street Residence

Architect:
Zach/de Vito Architecture

Location:
San Francisco, CA, United States

Photos:
© **Zach/de Vito Architecture**

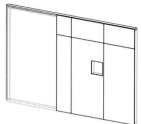
Exterior wall panel 1-6

CNC manufacturing in Forma factory

Digital model used for fabrication

Panel installation

This house is an example of how to create a modern, sustainable, and urban prefab home without compromising the final design.

1. Entry
2. Garage
3. Master suite
4. Bathroom
5. Guest room
6. Kitchen
7. Dining room
8. Living room
9. Sitting room
10. Family room
11. Bedroom
12. Laundry
13. Deck
14. Mechanical

Axonometric of the stair

Longitudinal sections

The open floor plan consists of two side volumes. The largest volume is three levels; the smaller volume has views of the south and benefits from strong light.

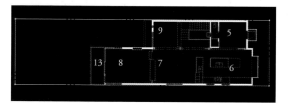

Second floor

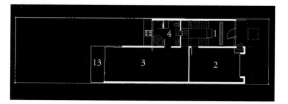

Ground floor

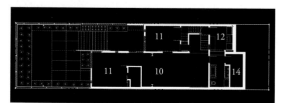

Basement floor

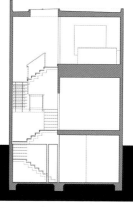

Transverse section

1. Entry
2. Garage
3. Master suite
4. Bathroom
5. Guest room
6. Kitchen
7. Dining room
8. Living room
9. Sitting room
10. Family room
11. Bedroom
12. Laundry
13. Deck
14. Mechanical

From the interior, the home has an all-encompassing view of the city and the bay. Steel and wood are the prevalent materials.

Damico House

Architect:
Karawitz Architecture

Location:
Le Mesnil-Saint Denis, France

Photos:
© Karawitz Architecture

Elevations

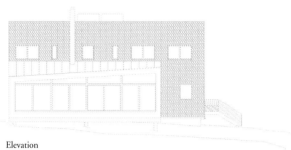

Elevation

Elevation

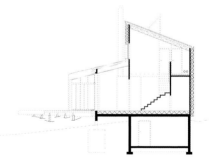

Cross section

This house is an energy-efficient house (it has the German Passivhaus label) and has a low environmental impact.

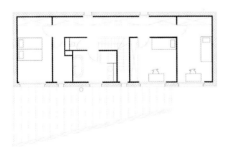

Floor plan

Mini House

Architect:
Jonas Wagell Design & Architecture

Location:
Stockholm, Sweden

Photos:
© Jonas Wagell Design & Architecture

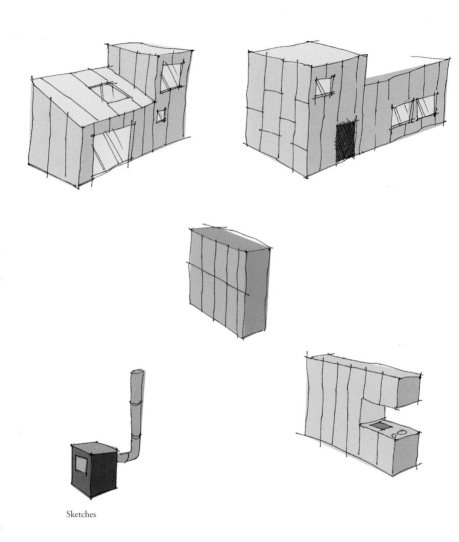

Sketches

Before designing this modular home prototype, Jonas Wagell carried out a preliminary study of the typology and possible modular construction systems.

The house, measuring only 15 m² (161 ft²), responds to a Swedish law that allows any home up to those exact measurments to be erected without permission from the government.

Villa Rotterdam

Architect:
Ooze Architects

Location:
Rotterdam, The Netherlands

Photos:
© Ooze Architects

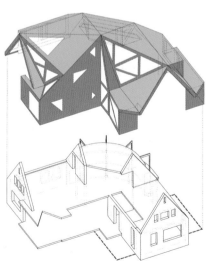

Axonometry

North elevation

East elevation

A new timber volume emerges next to the brick
façade of the original house and has triangular
windows with an unusual composition.

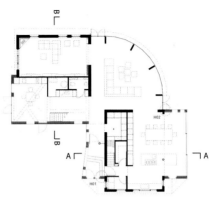

Ground floor plan

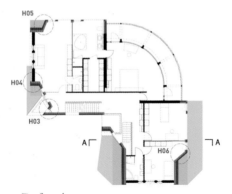

First floor plan

Ooze Architects undertook this restoration, transforming the old house into a home with modern lines that integrates techniques to achieve energy efficiency.

Modular House

Architect:
A-Cero

Location:
mobile

Photos:
© A-Cero

A-Cero Architects have developed a series of prefabricated houses based on modular architecture in order to provide housing at lower prices.

A-Ring House

Architect:
Atelier Tekuto

Location:
Kanazawa, Japan

Photos:
© Toshihiro Sobajima

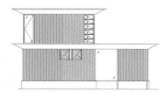

North elevation

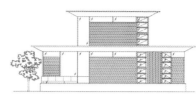

East elevation

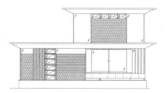

South elevation

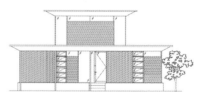

West elevation

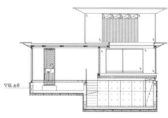

∇GL±0

Section

This house, which has an aluminum frame, is designed to function as a large radiator. The rings are designed to heat or cool the interior of the house depending on the season.

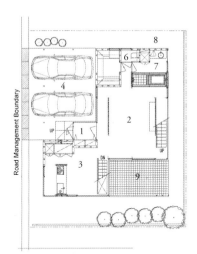

Ground floor plan

Basement plan

1. Entry
2. Living room
3. Kitchen/Dining room
4. Garage
5. Storeroom
6. Toilet
7. Sanitary
8. Green curtains
9. Terrace
10. Bedroom
11. Void
12. Roof garden

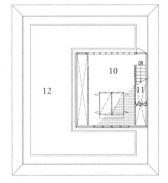

First floor plan

The house uses the power of geothermal energy and other active systems such as solar panels, a green roof, and rainwater collection systems.

The aluminum frames make use of underground heat to bring it into the interior of the house for irradiation.

Joshua Tree

Architect:
Hangar Design Group

Location:
mobile

Photos:
© Hangar Design Group

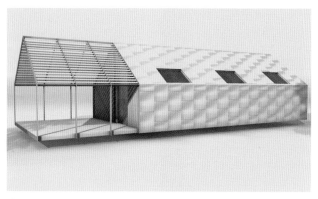

Elevation

Floor plan

Hangar Design Group designed Joshua Tree as
a mobile home that offers a workable solution
without sacrificing style.

263

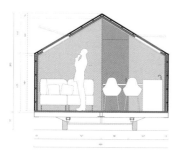

Cross sections

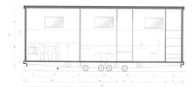

Longitudinal section

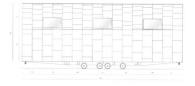

Side exterior model

Joshua Tree has the style of a modern country home or mountain refuge. The house is mobile, it can be placed wherever it is best suited and covers 34 m² (365 ft²).

The interior wood cladding promotes a high degree of insulation against the extreme outdoor temperatures.

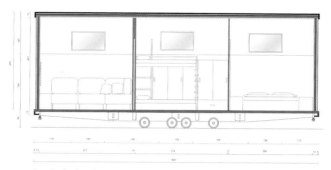

Longitudinal section

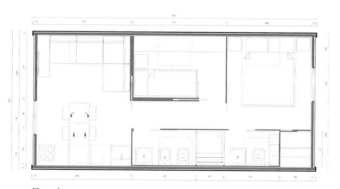

Floor plan

The interior layout includes a bedroom with a double bed, a bedroom with two single beds, two bathrooms, a kitchen, and a living room.

Qubic Student Housing Units

Architect:
HVDN Architecten

Location:
Amsterdam, The Netherlands

Photos:
© Luuk Kramer

Façade North

Façade South

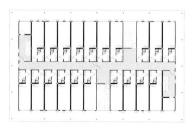

First floor

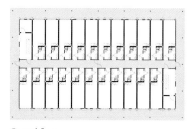

Ground floor

This student residence is composed of 715 small homes with a capacity for 1000 students.

The project was built in twelve months using prefabricated units as a container, which creates a façade of different colors.

Módulo 10x10

Architect:
stación-ARquitectura

Location:
Monterrey, México

Photos:
© Ana Cecilia Garza Villarreal

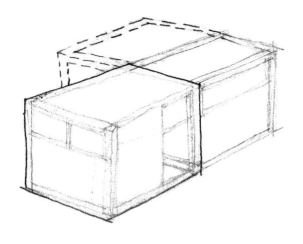

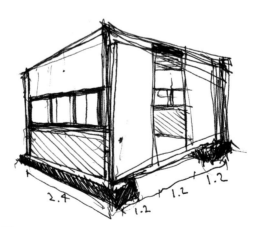

Esbozos

This project examines the possibilities of an
alternative construction system with materials and
economic construction methods.

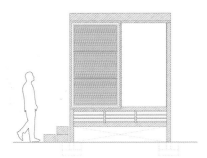

Elevations

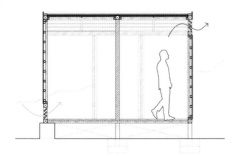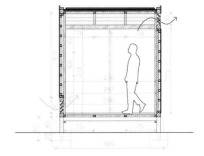

Bioclimatic diagrams

Fiberglass panels from other projects were used
for the construction and were transformed into a
flexible modular system.

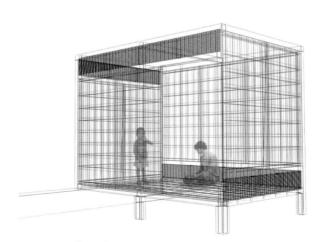

Perspective

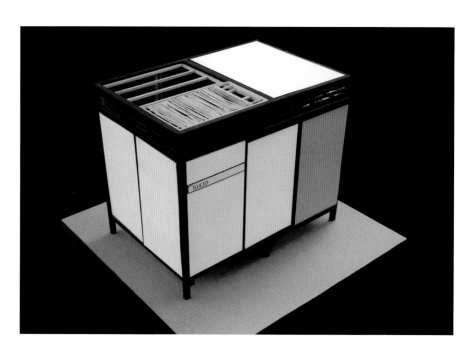

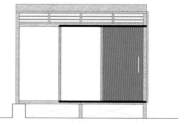
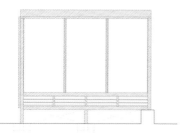

Elevations

Watershed

Architect:
Erin Moore

Location:
Wren, OR, United States

Photos:
© Gary Tarleton

This home was built from different prefabricated parts that were easy to assemble. The design consists of a steel-reinforced wooden frame and a polycarbonate roof.

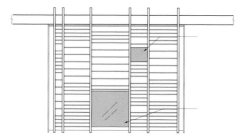

West elevation

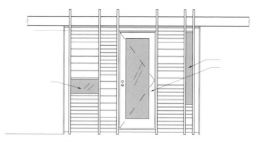

East elevation

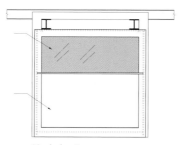

North elevation

There are numerous wide openings in the
structure through which to contemplate the birds
or find inspiration for writing.

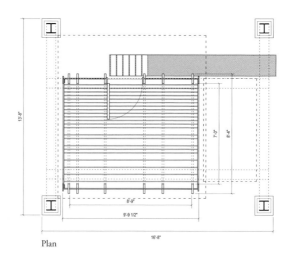

Plan

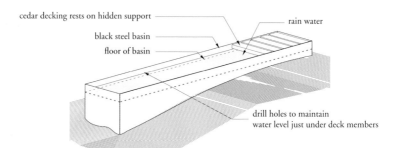

cedar decking rests on hidden support

rain water

black steel basin

floor of basin

drill holes to maintain
water level just under deck members

Trough for collecting water

A groove cut lengthways into the roof enables
rainwater to be collected.

The main feature of the interior is its simplicity. The most prominent space is occupied by a desk where the owner, a writer by profession, can find inspiration for his work.

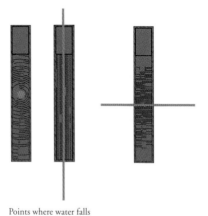

Points where water falls

Rucksack House

Architect:
Stefan Eberstadt

Location:
Leipzig and Cologne, Germany

Photos:
© Frank Motz, Claus Bach, Stefan Eberstadt, Hana Schäfer, Hans-Günter Schäfer, Thomas Taubert, Silke Koch

The interior furniture folds out to provide a range of different surfaces, such as a sleeping platform, a table, or a bench.

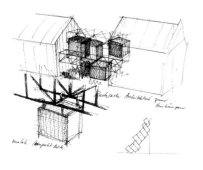

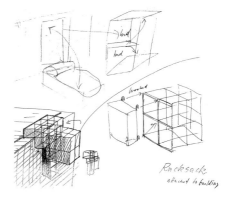

Skecthes

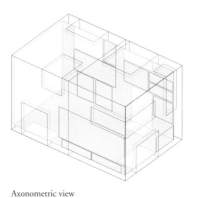

Axonometric view

The approximate weight of the cube is 1,100
kg/1.2 tons. When the furniture is folded away,
the interior lines are only broken by the windows.

The cube provides a transition between two environments: a private space that floats inside a public one.

Measurements of the different parts which make up the prototype

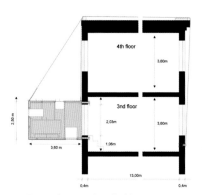

Rear anchoring with steel cable section

The volume measures 250 × 250 × 360 cm/ 99 × 99 × 142 in. The materials used to build it are very affordable.

MTGH

Architect:
Philippe Barriere Collective

Location:
mobile

Photos:
© renderings by Barriere Collective

Construction models

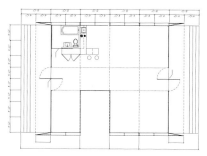

Plan of basic model - Option 1

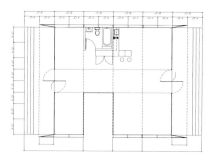

Plan of basic model - Option 2

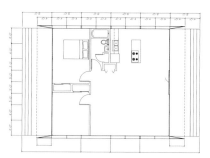

Plan of basic model with two bedrooms

MTGH modules are designed to be installed
wherever they are needed, particularly in
situations where temporary housing is required.

The basic modules are sold with or without a roof cantilever. The main entrance to the home is through double pivot doors.

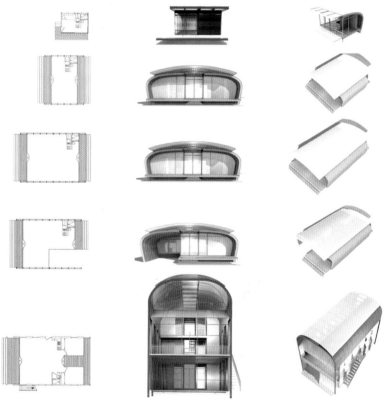

Possible combinations of modules (plans, elevations, and views in perspective)

First floor (module 1)

Second floor (module 2)

Third floor (module 3)

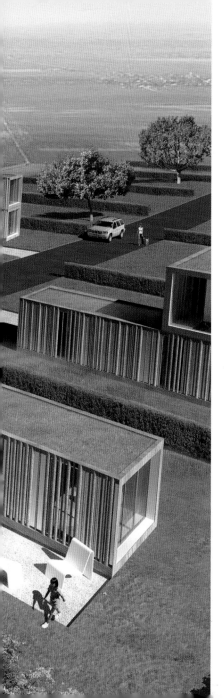

Evolutiv House

Architect:
Olgga Architects

Location:
Grenoble, France

Photos:
© Patrick Blanc, Pauline Turmel

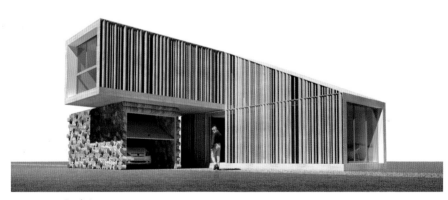

Renderings

This prototype was originally shown at the
Grenoble Innovations Fair. The aim was to build
a low-cost home made up of two prefabricated
modules.

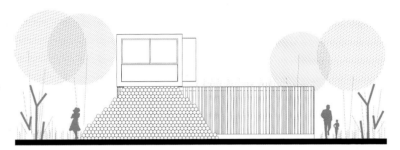

Longitudinal elevation

1. Sleeping area
2. Wood heap
3. Storage box
4. Living area

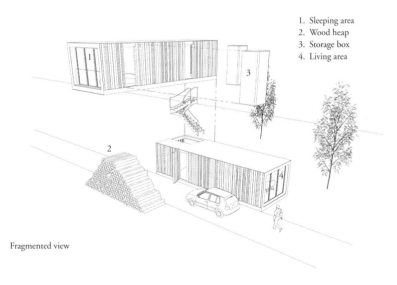

Fragmented view

One possible combination is to stack the two volumes to obtain a two-story rectangular home.

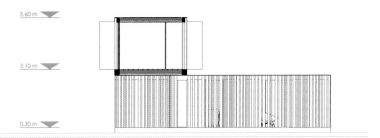

5.60 m

3.10 m

0.30 m

Section A-A

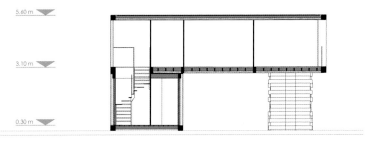

5.60 m

3.10 m

0.30 m

Section B-B

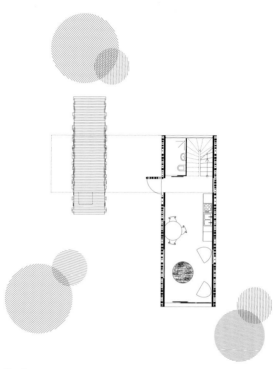

First floor

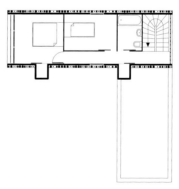

Second floor

The layout offers greater privacy on the upper level. The master bedroom and living area face south to benefit from more daylight.

House n° 19

Architect:
Korteknie Stuhlmacher Architekten

Location:
Utrecht, The Netherlands

Photos:
**© Christian Kahl, Korteknie Stuhlmacher
Architecten**

There are two doors on the sides that open like drawbridges. The other openings are glazed expanses framed in wood that are embedded into the building.

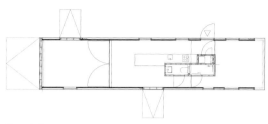

General plan

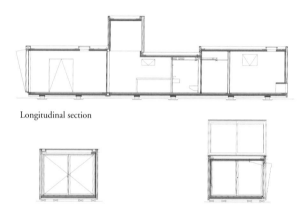

Longitudinal section

Cross section

Partial section

The design is based on a container. One of the end walls can be lowered to operate as a ramp or terrace. The volume measures 18 × 4 × 3.2 m/60 × 13 × 10.5 ft.

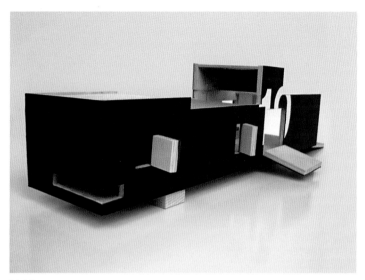

Model

General plan

House on Essex Street

Architect:
Andrew Maynard Architects

Location:
Brunswick, Australia

Photos:
© Peter Bennetts, Dan Mahon

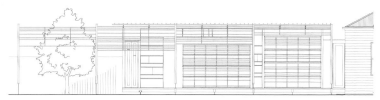

North elevation

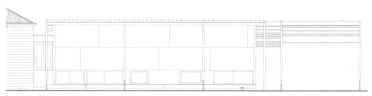

South elevation

East elevation

Located in a suburban area, this building is
inspired by Japanese interior design with its use of
natural materials (wood) and folding doors that
resemble screens.

Longitudinal elevation with sections

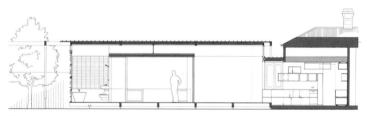

North longitudinal section

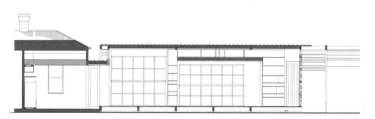

South longitudinal section

This new building is closed to the exterior by glass
façades and a double latticed skin in cedar wood.

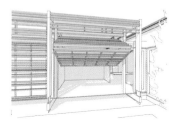
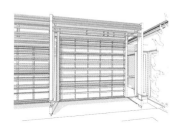

Views of the exterior in perspective

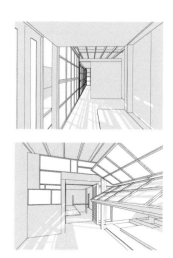

View of the interior in perspective

The main eco-friendly measures incorporated are its bioclimatic design, which enhances solar gain, and the use of recycled materials.

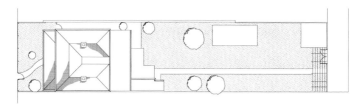

Plan of existing roof

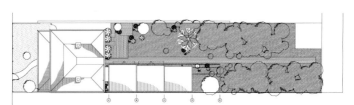

Plan of proposed roof

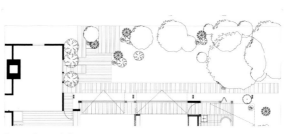

Proposed general plan

Burst 003

Architect:
Jeremy Edmiston, Douglas Gauthier/System Architects

Location:
North Haven, Australia

Photos:
© Floto + Warner

Burst is a good alternative to mass-produced models. It suggests varied solutions to expand geometries and forms, in order to create a home with guaranteed quality.

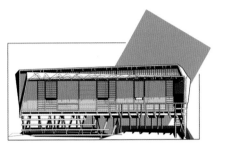

North elevation

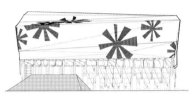

South elevation

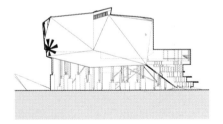

East elevation

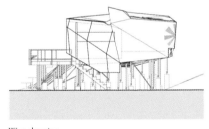

West elevation

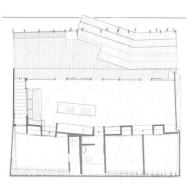

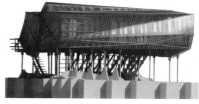

Rendering

Plan

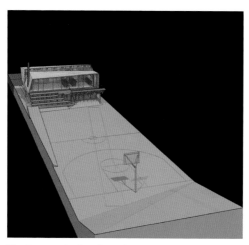

View in perspective from the north

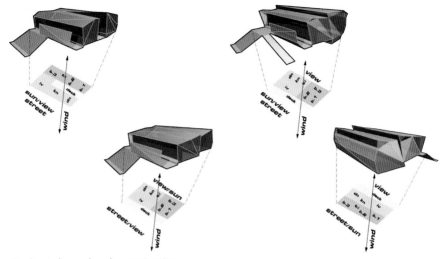

Bio-climatic diagram depending on orientation

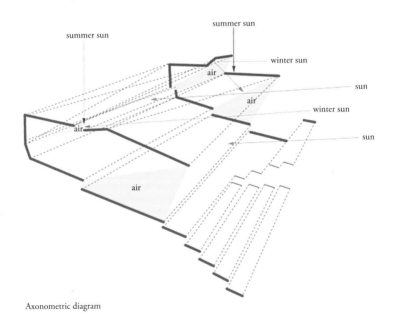

summer sun

summer sun

winter sun

air

air

sun

winter sun

air

sun

air

Axonometric diagram

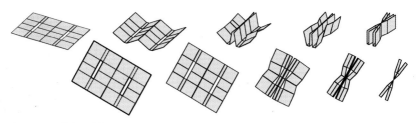

Axonometria of ribs and joints

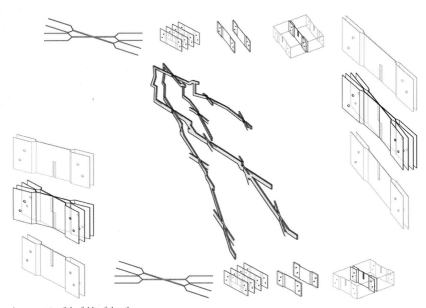

Axonometria of the folds of the ribs

The structure consists of a series of laser-cut
plywood ribs with a thickness of 25 mm/1 in.

Each rib was previously numbered and cut depending on its position. The floor structure is completed with two 12-mm/0.5-in. layers of plywood finished in resin.

Visualization of the roof

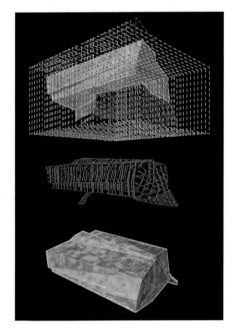

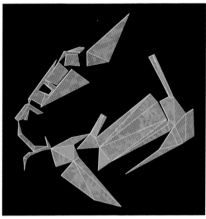

Visualization of the cladding

Visualization of the structure and cladding

House of Steel and Wood

Architect:
Ecosistema Urbano Arquitectos

Location:
Ranón, Spain

Photos:
© Emilio P. Doiztua

The northern façade is protected by an anterior space and a wind blocking lattice window.

Longitudinal elevation

Transversal elevation

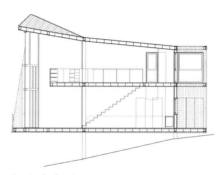

Longitudinal section

The double height void was not designed for reasons of space or composition; instead, it is an essential bioclimatic strategy for regulating the temperature inside the home.

Structure in detail

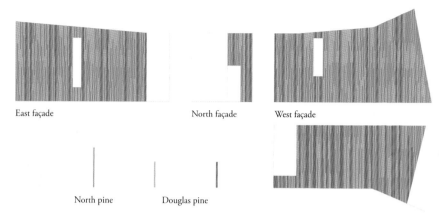

East façade

North façade

West façade

North pine   Douglas pine

Detail of wooden wall

Detail of shuttered wall

Laminated steel profiles are combined to form a prism shape that juts out at an angle on the southern facade.

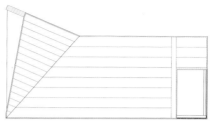

Roof

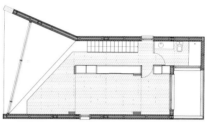

Second floor

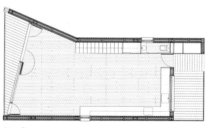

First floor

The exterior is covered in 35-mm/1.4-in. thick tongue and groove siding. The same material is used on interior walls, floors, and ceilings.

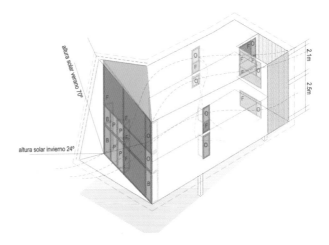

altura solar verano 70°

altura solar invierno 24°

2.1m

2.5m

Bio-climatic diagram

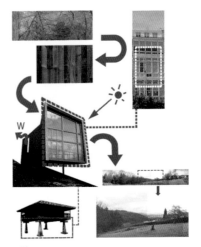

W

Ideogram

Solar incidence is blocked by means of a system of gaps in different positions. These act to regulate thermal comfort in response to the local microclimate.

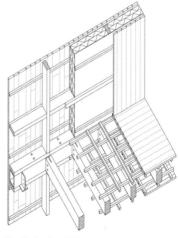

Detail of wall and slab

Nomadhome

Architect:
Hobby A. Schuster & Maul, Gerold Peham

Location:
Seekirchen am Wallersee, Austria

Photos:
© Marc Haader

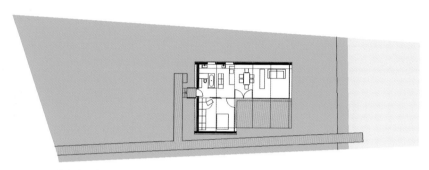

Location plan

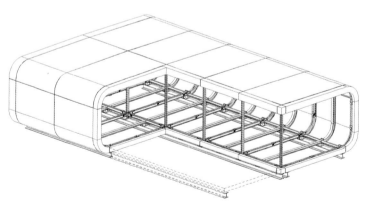

Axonometric view

This Nomadhome is located on the outskirts of the Austrian town of Seekirchen. The project is provisional, as the site is rented.

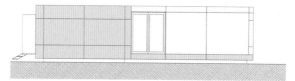

South-west elevation

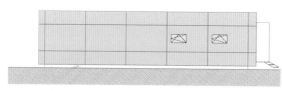

North-east elevation

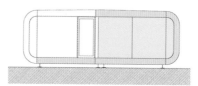

South-east elevation

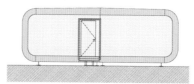

North-west elevation

The architects embodied the chameleonic and nomadic nature of the program through the simplicity with which the modules are assembled and disassembled.

The architects envisaged a future with communities or towns formed by a succession of Nomadhomes in which their tenants are the true nomads of the 21st century.

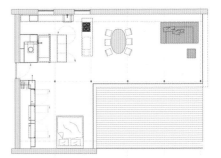

Plan of basic house

Ref-Ring

Architect:
Yasuhiro Yamashita/Atelier Tekuto

Location:
Zushi, Japan

Photos:
© Makoto Yoshida

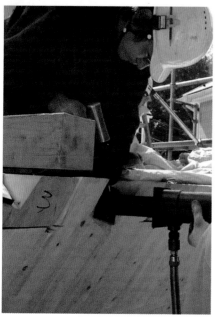

Location plan

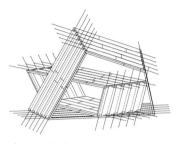

Axonometric view

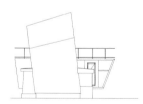

Elevations

The four sources of inspiration for the architects were reflection, materials, abstraction, and sensorial perception.

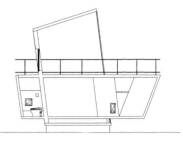

Sections

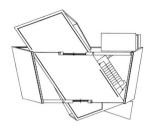

Second floor

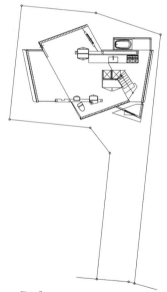

First floor

The floor structure has a surface area of 127 m2/1,370 sq. ft. The use of wood on interior surfaces provides an organic warmth that may be perceived as a little unwelcoming, depending on the occupant.

Hedge Building

Architect:
Atelier Kempe Thill Architects & Planners

Location:
Rostock, Germany

Photos:
© Ulrich Schwarz

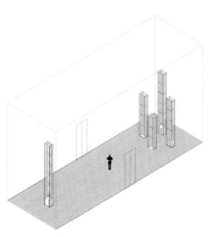

Axonometry of the video installation

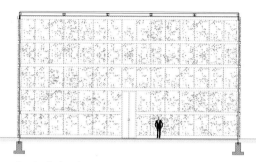

Longitudinal section

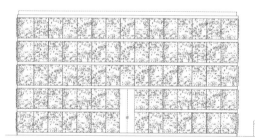

Longitudinal elevation

This volume has a rectangular geometry measuring 20 m/66 ft. in length with a height of 10 m/33 ft. The structure is anchored by the four wooden columns forming the corners of the building.

The interior is illuminated by the filtered light coming through the roof, giving the structure a feel that resembles a traditional museum.

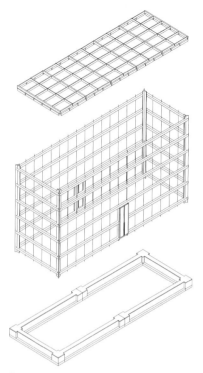

Fragment view

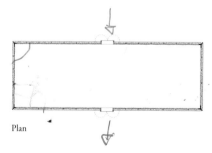

Plan

The building has three main parts: the base, which serves as an anchoring system; the hedges that serve as walls; and the clear polycarbonate roof.

The design for this "intelligent screen" where ivy can grow made this cool natural space possible in a relatively short time.

The "intelligent screen" comprises a series of identical elements that highlight the industrial feel of the building.

Renderings

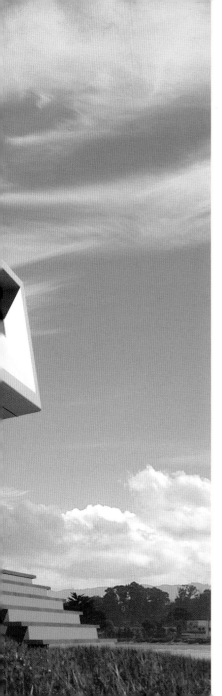

Zerohouse

Architect:
Specht Harpman

Location:
suitable for occupation during the whole year between latitudes 36° N and 36° S. Between 47° N and 47° S partial occupation is recommended

Photos:
© Renderings by Devin Keyes, Frank Farkash, Scott Specht

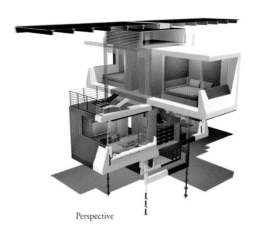

Perspective

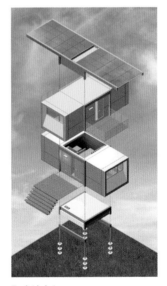

Exploided view

ZeroHouse can be installed anywhere, given
that it is suspended over a four-point anchoring
system that requires no earthmoving.

This model, designed for four adults, features a
bathroom, kitchen, and living and dining areas.

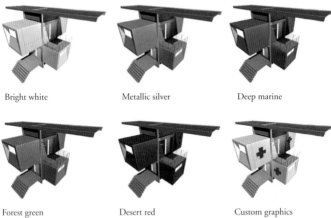

Bright white

Metallic silver

Deep marine

Forest green

Desert red

Custom graphics

ZeroHouse is suitable for protected natural
spaces, or places where permanent foundations
are not permitted.

House in Redondo Beach

Architect:
DeMaria Design Associates

Location:
Redondo Beach, CA, United States

Photos:
© Andre Movsesyan, Christian Kienapfel

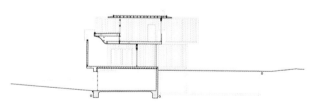

Transversal section

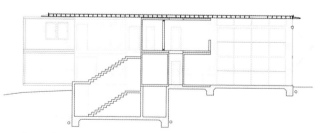

Longitudinal section

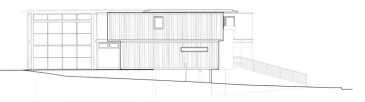

North elevation

South elevation

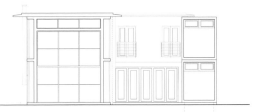

East elevation

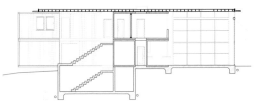

West elevation

The living area has a maximum height of 6 m/20 ft. and is separated from the exterior by folding doors similar to those used for hangars.

Second floor

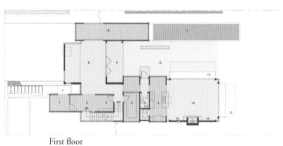

First floor

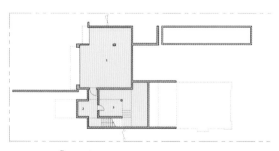

Basement

70% of the building work was carried out in a factory. This building technique enables time and cost to be controlled without compromising quality.

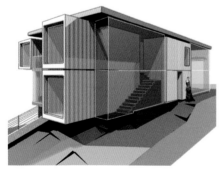

Rendering

Sustainable Prototype

Architect:
**Studio 804 (University of Kansas School of
Architecture and Urban Planning)**

Location:
Greensburg, KS, United States

Photos:
© Studio 804

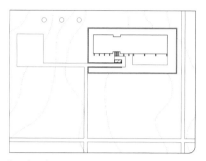

Location plan

South elevation

West elevation

Students participated in the building of the prototype, assisted by specialist tradespersons. Building time was 90 days.

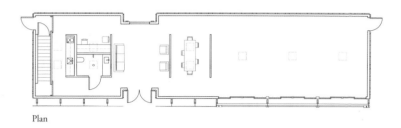

Plan

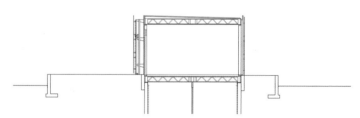

Transversal section

The building has a rectangular floor plan and comprises a main conference or exhibition room, a reception area, and a bathroom. There is also a basement.

Wildalpen Mountain Campus

Architect:
Holzbox

Location:
Wildalpen, Austria

Photos:
© Birgit Koell

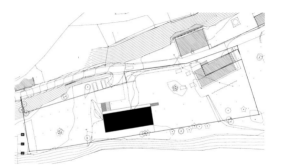

Location plan

North elevation

West elevation

East elevation

The usable surface area is 245 m²/2,637 sq. ft. divided into five apartment modules, which sleeps six or seven people, and a common room with a kitchen of almost 36 m²/388 sq. ft.

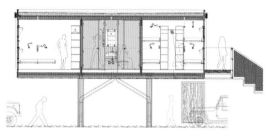

Longitudinal section of module-apartment

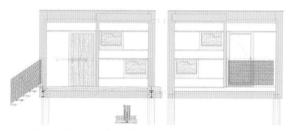

Transversal sections of module-apartment

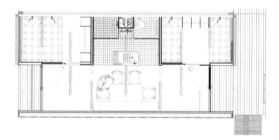

Plan of module-apartment

The layout provides each of the bedrooms with natural light. The apartment modules have covered open areas on the east façade.

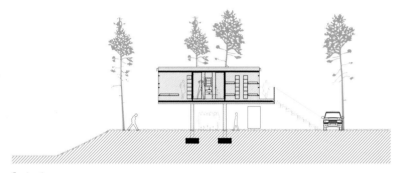

Section 1

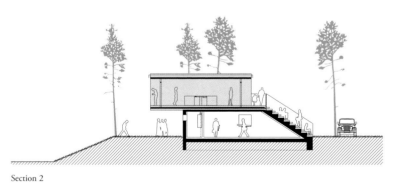

Section 2

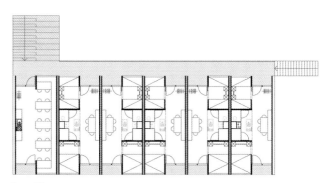

Second floor

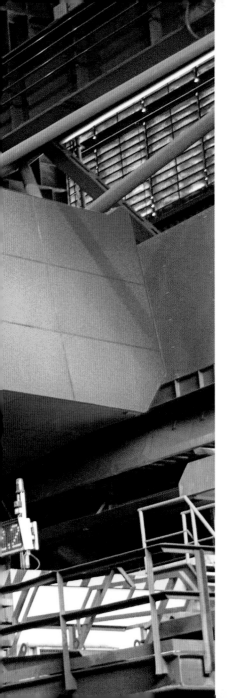

Visitors Platform

Architect:
Caramel Architekten, Friedich Stiper

Location:
Linz, Austria

Photos:
© Caramel Architekten

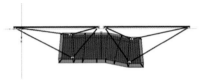

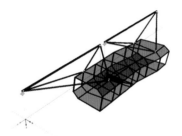

3D view of the roof and the suspention points

Structure in 3D

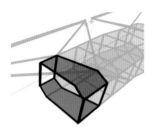

Standard module in 3D

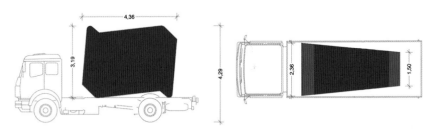

Illustration of transport of module using truck

These prefabricated modules can be transported by truck and assembled on-site. Their form and final layout depend on the client's needs.

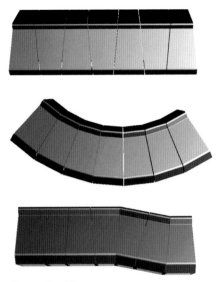

Concept of modular structure

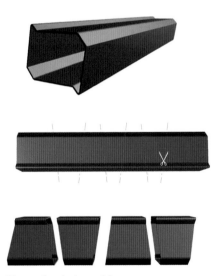

Diagram of production modules

Standard module with furnishings in perspective

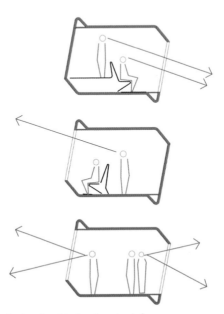

Section of possible views from the platform

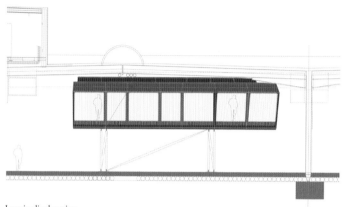

Longitudinal section

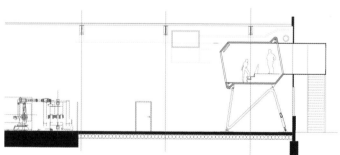

Transversal section

Once assembled, the modules form a platform of variable length. A walkway with a glass railing separates the platform from the stands.

Refugio Los Canteros

Architect:
dRN

Location:
Farellones, Chile

Photos:
© Felipe Camus

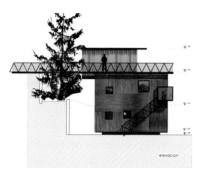

North elevation

East elevation

West elevation

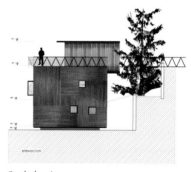

South elevation

The house is situated in a pre-existing slope, bounded by two stone retaining walls that define the plane.

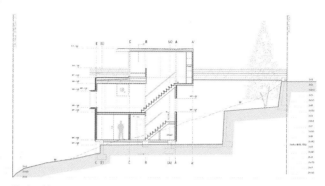

Section AA

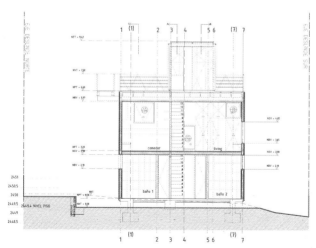

Section DD

The glare that the mountain light produces, as well as heat loss from the windows, is controlled by the contained interiors and minimal openings.

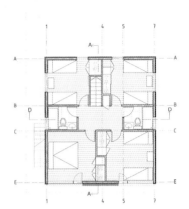

First level floor

Second level floor

Terrace level floor

The architects opted for a metal skeleton of pre-sized columns and beams to minimize the cost and construction time of the work.

Magic Box

Architect:
Jun Ueno/Magic Box

Location:
Palos Verdes, CA, United States

Photos:
© Magic Box

Section

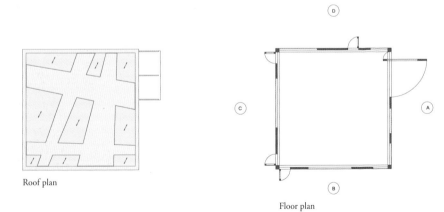

Roof plan

Floor plan

The structure can be transported by truck and has been designed to create a self-sufficient home. During the day, the glass façade allows light to enter.

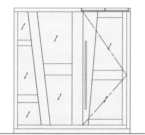

Elevation A

Elevation B

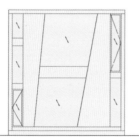

Elevation C

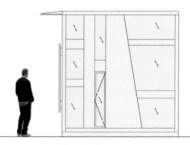

Elevation D

Fincube

Architect:
Studio Aisslinger

Location:
Ritten, Italy

Photos:
© Studio Aisslinger

Renderings

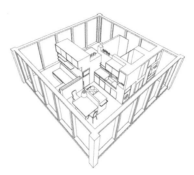

Floor plan

Fincube has a floor space of 47 m² (505 ft²) and is distributed according to the typical functions of a home-bedroom.

Local wood is used, and the home is designed to
be dismantled and rebuilt elsewhere.

Casa 205

Architect:
H Arquitectes

Location:
Vacarisses, Spain

Photos:
© Starp Estudi

Longitudinal section

Cross section

This house sits on land that slopes steeply with many trees and undergrowth that should be preserved.

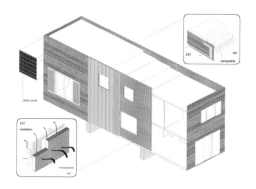

Axonometry

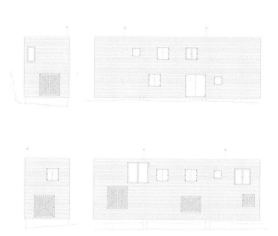

Elevations

The structural system allows for a reduction in weight, material, and embodied energy and, as a result, CO_2 emissions are associated with the foundations and structure.

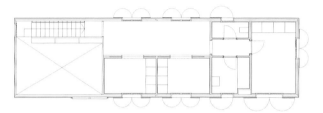

First floor plan

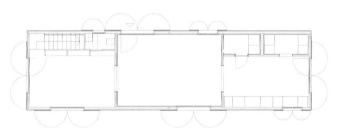

Ground floor plan

The interior layout is based on a linear sequence of spaces with large openings for sliding door and free spaces between them.

U+A House

Architect:
Neil M. Denari Architects

Location:
mobile

Photos:
© renderings by Neil M. Denari Architects

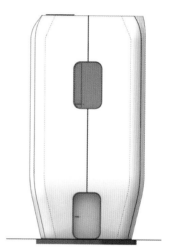

Elevation 1

Elevation 2

Vancouver-based Useful + Agreeable (U+A)
joined forces with architectural firm NMDA to
respond to the emerging market in prefabricated
homes for design-conscious consumers.

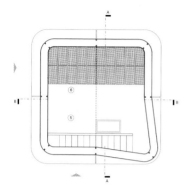

Cover roof/third floor

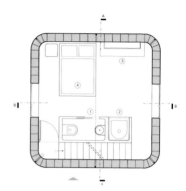

Second floor

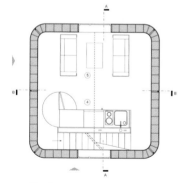

First floor

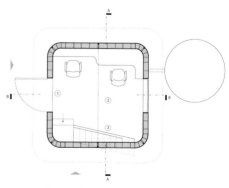

Ground floor

Their system, which is comprised of exterior siding and interior finishes, is similar to the technology used in aircraft wings. It provides a rigid skin that is also compact and lightweight.

Assembly sequence

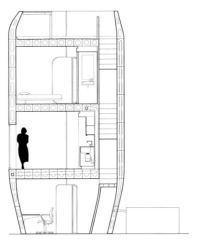

Section A-A

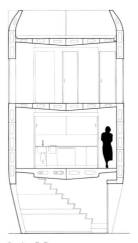

Section B-B

The prototype is clad in lightweight aluminum panels with an aeronautical design. The roof terrace can be used for installing solar panels and a rainwater harvesting system.

Maronaz

Architect:
RozO Architectes

Location:
La Possession, La Réunion, France

Photos:
© RozO Architectes

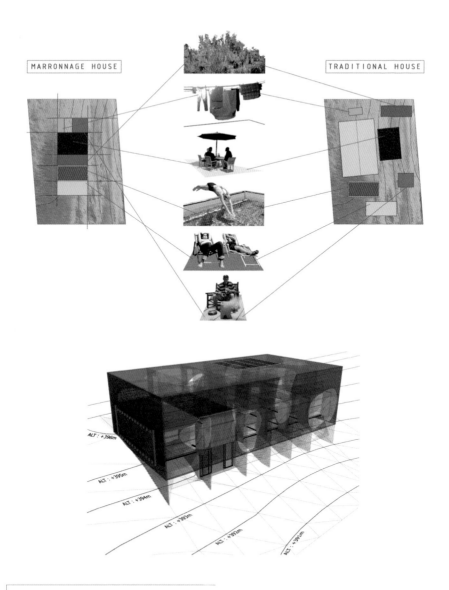

The enclosures created from welded metal mesh offer maximum natural ventilation and visual permeability to the exterior.

The building makes use of the concrete core of the swimming pool. This is the support from which the other structural components are developed.

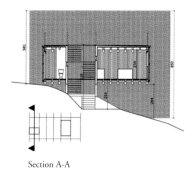

Section A-A

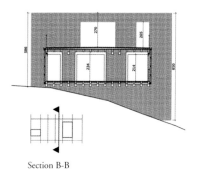

Section B-B

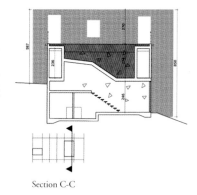

Section C-C

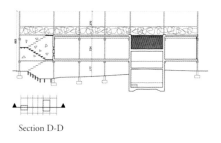

Section D-D

The existence of the external plastic mesh enables
the floor under the roof to be inhabitable. This
is where the swimming pool and main relaxation
areas are located.

Renderings of the diferent views from inside

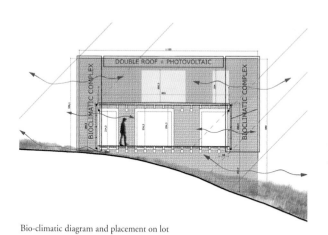

Bio-climatic diagram and placement on lot

The architect made the decision to adapt the home to its climate and terrain, which is particularly important when taking into account that these conditions are often not respected on islands such as this one.

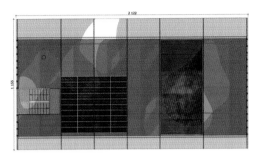

Roof

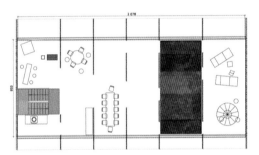

Second floor

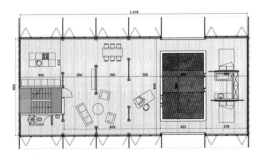

First floor

There is a close relationship between the home and the surrounding savannah, which, among other positives, serves to protect the house from potential damage that can be caused by hurricanes.

Casa Larga

Architect:
Daniele Claudio Taddei

Location:
Brissago, Switzerland

Photos:
© Bruno Helbling

East elevation

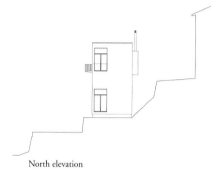

North elevation

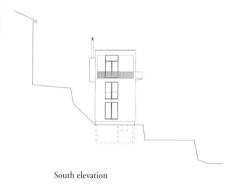

South elevation

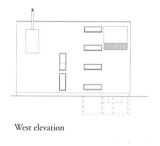

West elevation

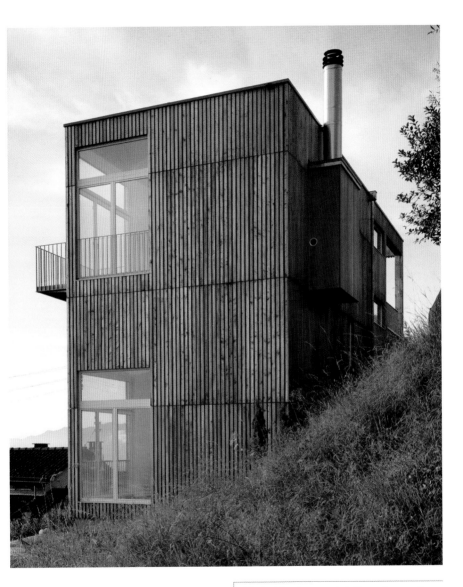

The building is accessed via the underground floor and is four stories high. The vertical lines dominate the façade where the rhythmic location of the windows stand out.

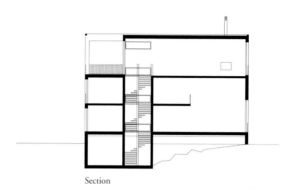

Section

Section atelier

This house, located in the middle of a vineyard, is perfectly integrated into the environment. Its elegant structure is reminiscent of farm buildings in the area.

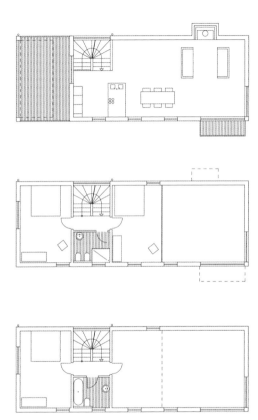

Floor plans

Inside, a staircase illuminated by natural light
connects all floors with a floating wooden
construction.

Four Cornered Villa

Architect:
Avanto Architects

Location:
Virrat, Finland

Photos:
© Kuvio Architectural Photography

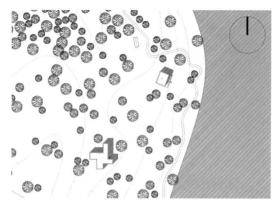

Site plan

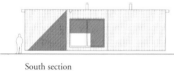

South section

East section

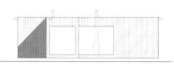

North section

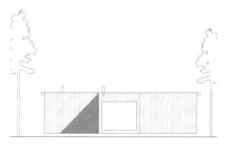

West section

The structure of the house is organized by the composition of four rectangular prisms with façades that open onto the landscape and are arranged in a cross.

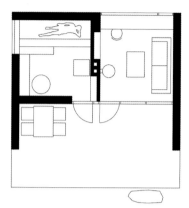

Floor plan

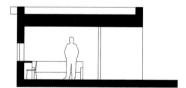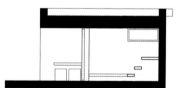

Sauna sections

The total area is 78 m² (839 ft²), plus the 24 m² (258 ft²) sauna, all of which is divided into four volumes to create an open but well defined space.

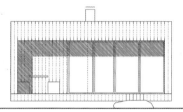

East elevation

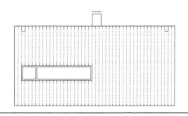

West elevation

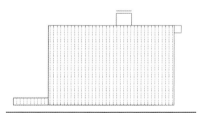

North elevation

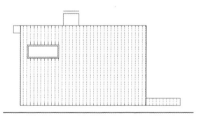

South elevation

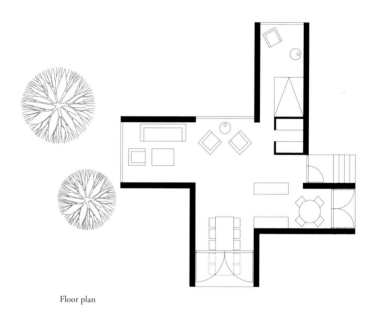

Floor plan

Each prism houses a different room: the living
room, dining room, kitchen, or bedroom.
At the intersection there is a visual interaction
of the spaces.

E Cube

Architect:
Carsten Jensen Architect

Location:
Qualicum Beach, Canada

Photos:
© Carsten Jensen

The structure was fabricated using CAD / CAM technology, and transported to the final destination to be assembled in situ.

Ground floor plan

1. Garage
2. Kitchen
3. Entry
4. Living
5. Dining
6. Bedroom

First floor plan

7. Study
8. Master bedroom
9. Outside deck
10. Green roof

The house was designed as an environmentally responsible building prototype and was produced by Jenesys Buildings.

The house has been designed to be energy-efficient: it has photovoltaic panels, a water collection system, and a green roof.

Happy House

Architect:
Carsten Jensen Architect

Location:
Bayfield, Canada

Photos:
© Pia Jensen

Site plan

In summer, the house benefits from cross
ventilation without the need for air conditioning.
Large windows provide a light and comfortable
interior.

could ntve been
true wcffall the Basket
to ultrapowreh
mind →s fer cantt euh me
that & Tris is me!

I amn't
guood forall e
cty↓

↓

[79]
Seu Fu
wuter
↓
no fwsc
tioleiott
belllla

↓

someday's
creer ultra
low flusch toiler ih ple mud.
↓ they cant see it.
↓
my given up was
hot his so I
hot his so I burgeans

Floor plan

1. Bedroom
2. Dining
3. Bedroom
4. Washroom
5. Entry
6. Kitchen
7. Sunroom
8. Living
9. Outside deck

506

The house was designed as a weekend retreat for an artist, overlooking Lake Huron near Bayfield, Ontario.

no solo
swid citolet
schiet to talk
gooed try to upunderlate
a wanp druageeante
all we talk
bonot pnd pride
vndeir apkeepon at

507

Rincon

Architect:
Marmol Radziner Prefab

Location:
mobile

Photos:
© **Tyler Boye**

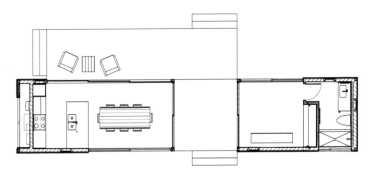

Floor plan

Rendering

Rincon's sliding walls enable cross ventilation. The porches also provide shade in summer, reducing the need for air conditioning.

The water heater operates only when required. This provides energy savings of up to 20% on conventional water heaters.

Gable Home

Architect:
University of Illinois

Location:
Urbana-Champaign, IL, United States

Photos:
© University of Illinois

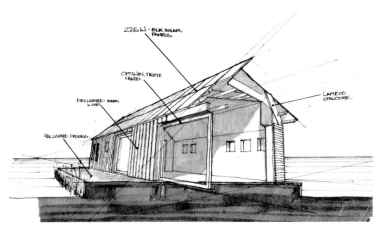

Sketch

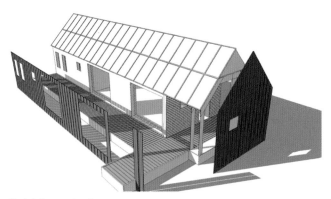

Exploded perspective view

The reuse of building materials from demolished structures—an old silo in this case—is yet another way of achieving sustainable architecture. Savings are made on materials, manufacturing, and transport.

3-D renderings

These 3D renderings show the simplicity of the design: the timber beams and the shape of the roof recall the architecture of the area's farms and barns.

Structure perspective

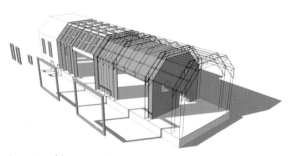

Perspective of the structure interior

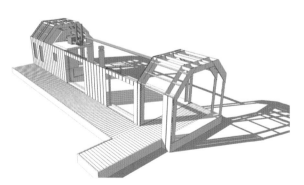

Perspective of reused timber boards

The south façade makes use of the sun with both direct and indirect strategies: glazed expanses let natural light and heat into the house.

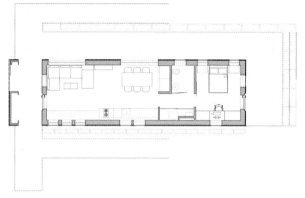

Floor plan

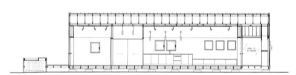

Longitudinal section

Cross section

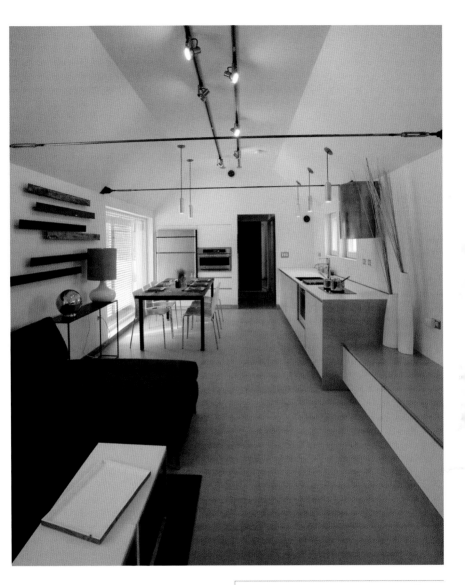

The floor plan and sections show the size of spaces. The layout can be varied to provide more bedrooms or additional spaces.

Martin Residence Addition

Architect:
@6 Architecture

Location:
Berkeley, CA, United States

Photos:
© Adrian Gregorutti

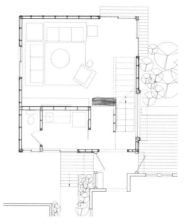

Upper level

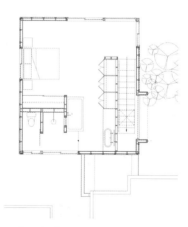

Lower level

The Martin residence was enlarged by adding a small, two-story space: a living area with one bathroom and one bedroom.

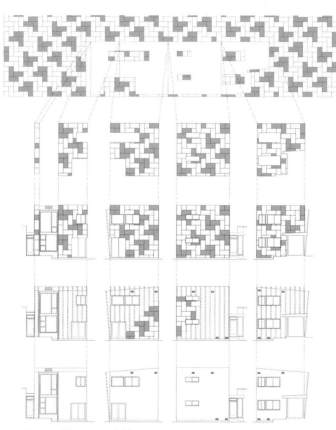

Diagram of fiber-cement cladding

The fiber cement panels were cut to precise measurements in the factory. They were laid over beams in a herringbone pattern.

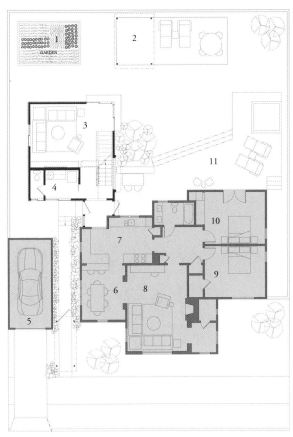

Ground floor plan

1. Garden
2. Patio
3. Family room
4. Laundry
5. Garage
6. Dining

7. Kitchen
8. Living
9. Bedroom
10. Bedroom
11. Deck

Cabinets, bathroom furnishings, and floors feature recyclable bamboo panels. The steps were made out of recycled wood.

Huis JP

Architect:
Change Architects

Location:
Bilthoven, The Netherlands

Photos:
© Pieter Kers/Change Architects

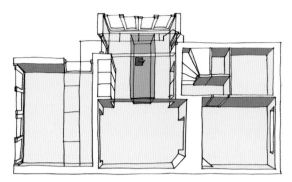

Floor plan

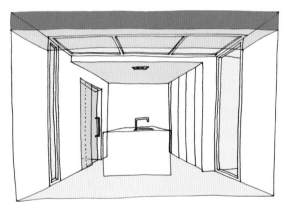

Perspective

This remodel took into account a number
of strategies for improving the conditions in
the home and to incorporate a number of
sustainability criteria into the architecture.

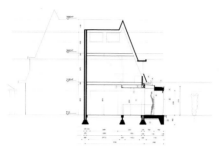

Cross section

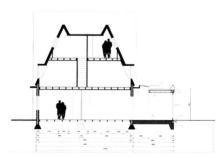

Longitudinal section

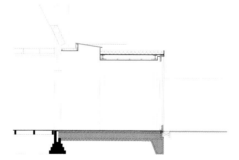

Addition construction detail

The new rooms increase the floor space, while
improving the insulation for the rest of the house.

The dark wood used on the façade is FSC-certified. The use of regulated material helps to prevent deforestation on the planet.

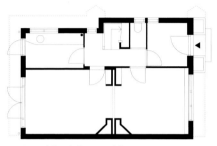

Ground floor before remodeling

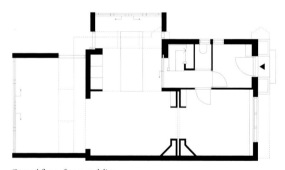

Ground floor after remodeling

The addition features a large amount of glass, providing light to common areas. This results in lower electricity use.

Taliesin Mod.Fab

Architect:
**Taliesin Design/Build Studio,
Office of Mobile Design**

Location:
Scottsdale, AZ, United States

Photos:
© Bill Timmerman

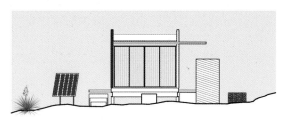

East elevation

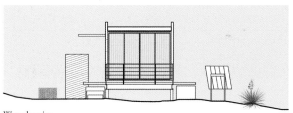

South elevation

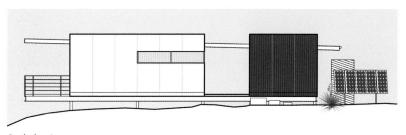

West elevation

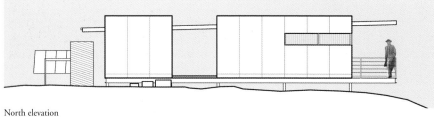

North elevation

The roof cantilever creates a porch area that offers shelter and shade. The glazed walls let in natural light for most of the day.

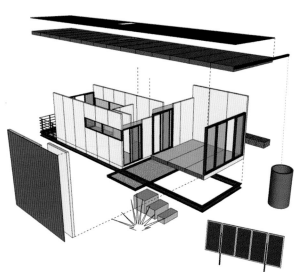

Diagram of the environmental features of the house

The photovoltaic array in the garden provides electricity to meet the occupants' needs.

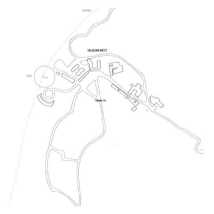

Site plan

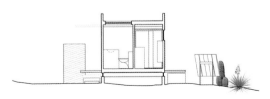

Cross section

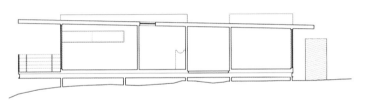

Longitudinal section

This residence was built using structural insulated panels (SIPs) for speed and savings, both in the factory and during assembly on-site.

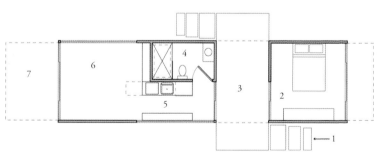

Floor plan

1. Entry/Stairs
2. Bedroom
3. Covered breezeway
4. Bath
5. Kitchen
6. Living room
7. Covered deck

itHouse

Architect:
Taalman Koch Architecture

Location:
Pioneertown, CA, United States

Photos:
© **Art Gray**

Site plan

Rendering

The architects placed a number of vinyl graphics over the glass walls to emphasize the idea that the house was integrated into the desert landscape surrounding it.

itHouse makes use of a series of prefabricated components to provide better control over building waste, the quality of workmanship and, in the end, the final result.

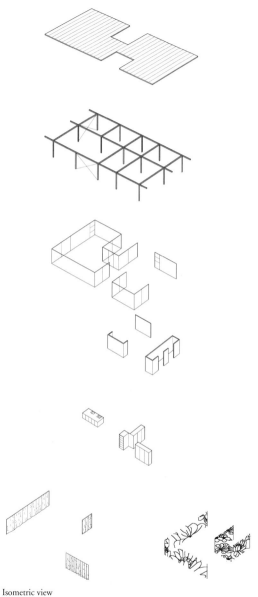

Isometric view

Solar panels were installed in the middle of the courtyard in order to provide shade at times of greater solar incidence.

Bridge House

Architect:
Max Pritchard Architect

Location:
Ashbourne, Australia

Photos:
© **Sam Noonan**

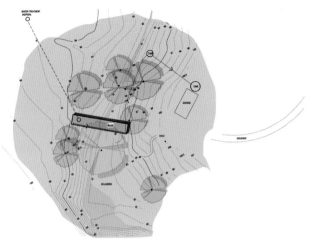

Site plan

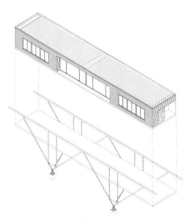

Axonometric view of the structure

The house is built over a metal structure. This placement means it has minimum impact on the site, given that there was no need to cut down trees or change the course of the stream.

The double glazing keeps in the heat entering through the north façade in winter, which is helpful because more sun enters through this side during the winter months in the southern hemisphere.

Steel panels and the surrounding trees protect the house from high temperatures during the summer months.

This structure supports a concrete slab over which the home, with dimensions a little over 100 m2/1,000 sq. ft., stands.

Floor plan

Residential Containers

Architect:
Petr Hájek Architekti

Location:
Prague, Czech Republic

Photos:
© Ester Havlova

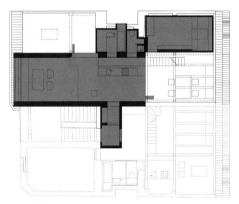

Lower level

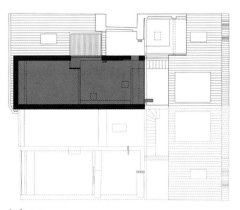

Loft space

The containers blend seamlessly with the
building. The large windows provide the
apartment with light and heat.

The apartment interior has two interconnected levels. The absence of partitions enables light to reach all the spaces, keeping the temperature even throughout the apartment.

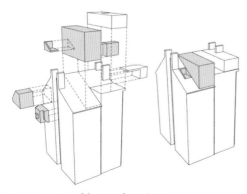

Axonometric view of the inserted containers

The loft space created in the apartment features
a small and comfortable reading room with views
of the exterior and the lower level. Repurposed
containers were remodelled with traditional
systems and materials and used for the bathroom.

Vermont Cabin

Architect:
Resolution: 4 Architecture

Location:
Jamaica, VT, United States

Photos:
© RES4

Prefabricated construction produces less impact on the environment, while building times are shortened and the need for machines and their operators is reduced.

The house stands in a small clearing where it receives direct sunlight. An adjoining path through the forest connects the house with the nearest town.

First floor plan

The layout of the house is very simple: an open plan kitchen and living-dining area, two bathrooms, and three bedrooms—one of which serves multiple purposes.

Restored Farmhouse

Architect:
Jeffrey McKean Architect

Location:
Claryville, NY, United States

Photos:
**© Keith Mendenhall/Jeffrey McKean
Architect**

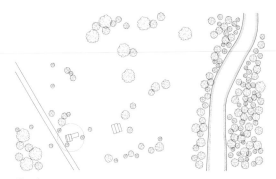

Site plan

Longitudinal section

Cross section

Salvaging wood and the use of FSC-certified
timber guarantee that natural resources are not
wasted.

The contrast between the materials used on the outer walls of the old farmhouse and the addition will mellow over time.

Lower level

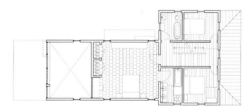

Upper level

Peconic Bay House

Architect:
Resolution: 4 Architecture

Location:
Shinnecock Hills, NY, United States

Photos:
© RES4

The siding of the main volume is cedar wood. Because they need very little treatment, natural materials like wood are the easiest to recycle or reuse.

3-D rendering

West elevation

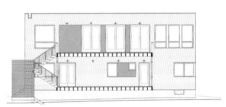

South elevation

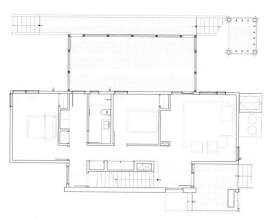

Lower level

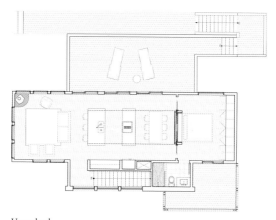

Upper level

This orientation offers the house the maximum
hours of daylight. Openings are larger on the
south façade where there is also a large deck and
glass-encased porch.

The kitchen separates the dining area from the
bedroom. Electricity is supplied by photovoltaic
panels and geothermal energy.

Berkshire House

Architect:
Resolution: 4 Architecture

Location:
West Stockbridge, MA, United States

Photos:
© RES4

Model

The modules were built in a factory, although final assembly was carried out on-site. Shortening the building time contributed to lower CO_2 emissions.

3-D renderings

24
25
26
28 84
29 80
41 4t 45
43 84 44
46 +47 48
30
60 100
400 80
70 60 5040
30 20 10
50

no iesehectic
cpall, so gyrand
tren if Dure
n'Pox Babetxe
Dight
forever
Urgeoft
awel-t-s
hol for
extruanv
that
emo
lounjiex
5g

Upper level

downts
fr pimnn
a
ecg
wat

Lower level

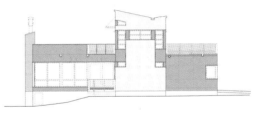

East elevation

West elevation

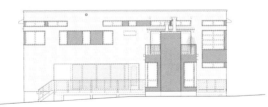

North elevation

South elevation

The glass expanses and two terraces on the upper level blur the boundaries between interior and exterior.

Bamboo was chosen as a floor covering owing to this natural material being very warm and durable.

Santa Monica PreFab

Architect:
Office of Mobile Design

Location:
Santa Monica, CA, United States

Photos:
© Laura Hull

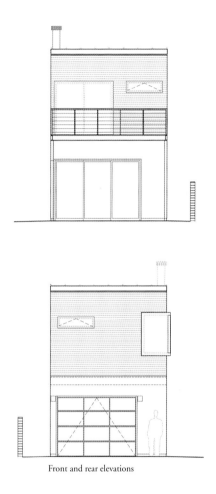

Front and rear elevations

The lower floor contains the garage, kitchen, and living area, while the upper floor contains the bedrooms and an office space.

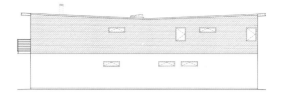

Side elevations

Second floor

First floor

1. Living/Dining
2. Kitchen
3. Garage
4. Bath
5. Laundry
6. Mechanical room
7. Storage
8. Bedroom
9. Bath
10. Office
11. Bath
12. Master bedroom

The Hardiplank fiber cement panels require little maintenance and are more durable than wood and stucco. They are also fire resistant.

Fab Lab House

Architect:
IAAC, MIT's CBA, Fab Lab

Location:
Madrid, Spain

Photos:
© Fab Lab House

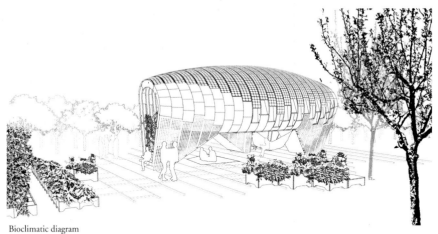

Bioclimatic diagram

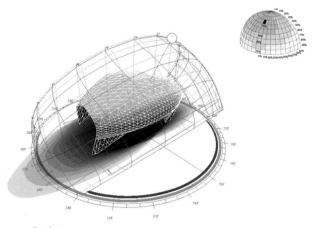

Rendering

The Fab Lab House is a self-sufficient house produced for the Solar Decathlon Europe 2010, by a group of organizations led by the Institute for Advanced Architecture Institute of Catalonia.

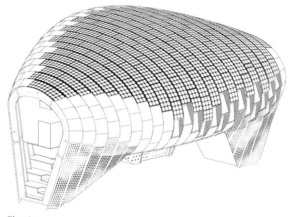

Elevation

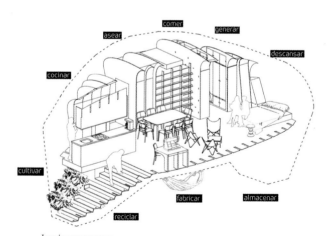

Interior axonometry

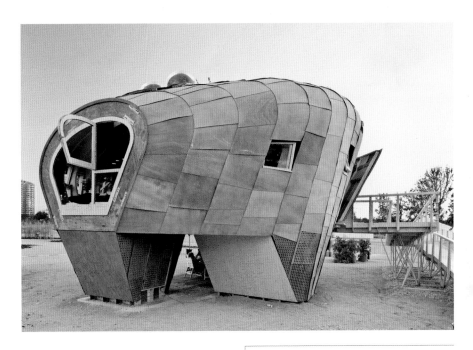

The objective was to design a solar house that produces maximum resources with minimal investment.

This is not a box with solar panels on the roof, but rather it integrates its physical structure with its energy production and the management of the information that it generates.

DIRECTORY

@6 Architecture
San Francisco, CA, United States
www.at-six.com

A-Cero
Madrid, Spain
www.a-cero.com

Add a Room
Tyresö, Sweden
www.addaroom.eu

Andrade Morettin Arquitetos
São Paulo, Brazil
www.andrademorettin.com.br

Andrew Maynard Architects
Melbourne, Australia
www.maynardarchitects.com

Arquitectura X
Quito, Ecuador
www.arquitecturax.com

Atelier Kempe Thill Architects & Planners
Rotterdam, The Netherlands
www.atelierkempethill.com

Atelier Tekuto
Tokyo, Japan
www.tekuto.com

Atelier Werner Schmidt
Trun, Switzerland
www.atelierwernerschmidt.ch

Avanto Architects
Helsinki, Finland
www.avan.to

Caramel Architekten
Vienna, Austria
www.caramel.at

Carsten Jensen Architect
London, Ontario, Canada
www.carstenjensenarchitect.com

Change Architects
Amsterdam, The Netherlands
www.changearchitects.nl

Daniele Claudio Taddei
Zurich, Switzerland
www.taddei-architect.com

DeMaria Design Associates
Manhattan Beach, CA, United States
www.demariadesign.com

dRN
Santiago, Chile
www.drn.cl

Ecosistema Urbano Arquitectos
Madrid, Spain
www.ecosistemaurbano.com

Erin Moore
erin@floatarch.com

FAR frohn&rojas
Berlin, Germany
Santiago, Chile
Los Angeles, CA, United States
www.f-a-r.net

FLOAT Architectural Research and Design
Portland, OR, United States
www.floatwork.com

Franz Architekten
Vienna, Austria
www.franz-architekten.at

H Arquitectes
Sabadell, Spain
www.harquitectes.com

Hangar Design Group
Mogliano Veneto, Italy
www.hangar.it

Hobby A. Schuster & Maul, Gerold Peham
Salzburg, Austria
www.nomadhome.com

HVDN Architecten
Amsterdam, The Netherlands
www.hvdn.nl

Holzbox
Innsbruck, Austria
www.holzbox.at

IAAC (Institute for Advanced Architecture of Catalonia), MIT's CBA, Fab Lab
Barcelona, Spain
www.fablabhouse.com

Jeffrey McKean Architect
New York, NY, United States
www.jeffreymckean.com

Jeremy Edmiston, Douglas Gauthier/System Architects
New York, NY, United States
www.systemarchitects.com

Jonas Wagell Design & Architecture
Stockholm, Sweden
www.jonaswagell.se

Jun Ueno/Magic Box
Palos Verdes, CA, United States
www.magicboxinusa.com

Karawitz Architecture
Paris, France
www.karawitz.com

KieranTimberlake Associates
Philadelphia, PA, United States
www.kierantimberlake.com

Kim Herforth Nielsen/3XN
Copenhagen, Denmark
www.3xn.dk

Korteknie Stuhlmacher Architecten
Rotterdam, The Netherlands
www.kortekniestuhlmacher.nl

Lars Frank Nielsen/One N
Åbyhøj, Sweden
www.onen.dk

Magnus Ståhl
Stockholm, Sweden
www.staahl.com

Manfred Adams, Huf Haus
Hartenfels, Germany
www.huf-haus.com

Marmol Radziner Prefab
Los Angeles, CA, United States
www.marmolradzinerprefab.com

Matthias R. Schmalohr
Bückeburg, Germany
www.schmalohrarchitect.com

Max Pritchard Architect
Adelaide, Australia
www.maxpritchardarchitect.com.au

Mitsutomo Matsunami Architect & Associates
Osaka, Japan
www.mma-design.com

M. J. Neal Architects
Austin, TX, United States
www.mjneal.com

MKD-Michelle Kaufmann Designs
Waltham, MA, United States
www.mkdesigns.com

Neil M. Denari Architects Inc.
Los Angeles, CA, United States
www.nmda-inc.com

Office of Mobile Design
Venice, CA, United States
www.designmobile.com

Olgga Architects
Paris, France
www.olgga.fr

Ooze Architects
Rotterdam, The Netherlands
www.ooze.eu.com

Oskar Leo Kaufmann, Albert Rüf
Dornbirn, Austria
www.olkruf.com

Petr Hájek Architekti
Prague, Czech Republic
www.hajekarchitekti.cz

Philippe Barriere Collective
www.philippebarrierecollective.com

Pich-Aguilera
Barcelona, Spain
www.picharchitects.com

Resolution: 4 Architecture
New York, NY, United States
www.re4a.com

Ronan & Erwan Bouroullec
Paris, France
www.bouroullec.com

RozO Architectes
Aubervilliers, France
www.rozo.archi.fr

Sander Architects
Los Angeles, CA, United States
www.sander-architects.com

Specht Harpman
Austin, TX, United States
www.zerohouse.net

stación-ARquitectura
San Pedro Garza García, NL, México
www.stacion-arquitectura.com

Stefan Eberstadt
Munich, Germany
stefan.eberstadt@stefaneberstadt.com

Studio 804
Lawrence, KS, United States
www.studio804.com

Studio Aisslinger
Berlin, Germany
www.aisslinger.de

Studio NL-D
Rotterdam, The Netherlands
www.studionl-d.com

Taalman Koch Architecture
Los Angeles, CA, United States
www.tkarchitecture.com

Taliesin Design/Build Studio
Scottsdale, Arizona, EE. UU.
www.taliesin.edu

University of Illinois
Urbana, IL, United States
www.illinois.edu

Zach/de Vito Architecture
San Francisco, CA, United States
www.zackdevito.com